Image Technologies in Canadian Literature

Narrative, Film, and Photography

P.I.E. Peter Lang

Bruxelles · Bern · Berlin · Frankfurt am Main · New York · Oxford · Wien

Canadian Studies

The series Canadian Studies examines the many facets of Canadian reality from a multidisciplinary perspective. Contributions from both the humanities and the social sciences are invited. The editor welcomes manuscripts whose primary object is "Canada" in the widest possible sense of the term. The series therefore covers a variety of fields such as literature, history, sociology, politics, economics, geography, law, media, museology, etc. as well as comparative studies.

One of the most innovative features of this series is its focus on the latest research conducted outside Canada. It therefore illuminates various aspects of the country in a new and significant manner and encourages a constant and innovative dialogue between Canadian scholars and the community of Canadian studies specialists worldwide.

Carmen Concilio & Richard J. Lane (eds.)

Image Technologies in Canadian Literature

Narrative, Film, and Photography

Canadian Studies
n° 17

The editors gratefully acknowledge
the financial support of the University of Turin.

Éditions scientifiques internationales
Brussels, 2009
1 avenue Maurice, B-1050 Bruxelles, Belgique
www.peterlang.com ; info@peterlang.com

Printed in Germany

ISSN 1781-3867
ISBN 978-90-5201-474-6
D/2009/5678/14

Library of Congress Cataloging-in-Publication Data
Image technologies in Canadian literature : narrative, film, and photography /
Carmen Concilio & Richard J. Lane (eds.).
p. cm. — (Etudes canadiennes ; no 17) Includes bibliographical references.
ISBN 978-90-5201-474-6
1. Canadian literature—20th century—History and criticism. 2. Literature and photography—Canada. 3. Photography in literature. 4. Visual perception in literature. 5. Literature and technology. I. Concilio, Carmen. II. Lane, Richard J.
PR9185.5.P59I43 2009 810.9'356—dc22 2008052709

CIP also available from the British Library, GB.

Bibliographic information published by "Die Deutsche Bibliothek"

"Die Deutsche Bibliothek" lists this publication in the "Deutsche Nationalbibliografie"; detailed bibliographic data is available on the Internet at <http://dnb.ddb.de>.

Contents

Acknowledgements

The editors would like to thank all those who made possible the cooperation agreement between The University of Turin, School of Modern Literatures and Languages, and Vancouver Island University, Faculty of Arts and Humanities. We would also like to thank: Professor Serge Jaumain, Faculty of Philosophy and Letters, Université Libre de Bruxelles, for supporting this project; Prof. Donatella Badin and Dr. Paola Brusasco for their patient reading sessions; Dr. Giusy Cutrì for the precious final editing and formatting of the manuscript; and Nicoletta Barbarito, responsible for Academic Relations at the Canadian Embassy in Rome and Professor Deborah Madsen, University of Geneva, for their constant support and suggestions.

C. C. and R. J. L.

Editors' Foreword

Image technologies, in this case photography and cinema, permeate contemporary Canadian Literature to the point of merging and blending with written texts so as to create hybrid, complex works of art. The present collection of essays explores precisely the encounter between CanLit and image technologies and tries to record this stereophony of bilingualism both across Canada and through a lively dialogue between Italian and Canadian scholars. Chapters cover acclaimed contemporary Canadian writers including: Michael Ondaatje, Daphne Marlatt (and the photographer Robert Minder), Ann-Marie MacDonald, Robert Kroetsch, Joseph Dandurand and the visual artist and writer Stan Douglas, while the film discussed here concerns the writer/singer Leonard Cohen.

Most, if not all, of the literary texts here analysed often translate or mirror (moving or frozen) images that emerge from the same body of authorial experience, thus creating a new textuality/visuality that engages the reader in modalities of dual, if not doubled, reading/interpreting of those works of art. A "slippage" from the written word to the visual world therefore captures the reader of both these essays and of the texts they tackle, transforming him/her into an interrogating, open eye/I. The articles by Lucia Boldrini, Jeffrey Orr, Simona Bertacco and Richard Lane in particular are concerned – among other topics – with this kind of active engagement that the texts require from readers while presenting some of Canada's most interesting contemporary writers and artists. From Walter Benjamin's philosophical and aesthetic paradigms of reproducibility and the mystery/magic of photography to Roland Barthes and Susan Sontag's paradigm of spectrality, all the essays here gathered try to "avoid recycling tired notions of postmodernism," as Richard Lane points out, by reconsidering theoretical categories such as Benjamin's "dialectical image" (R. Lane); or "intersemiotic translation" (J. Orr); or Lacan's "anamorphosis" (L. Boldrini). And here "slippage" is both keyword and privileged modality that allows movement and metamorphosis between genres, techniques, narrators/characters' status (Keith Harrison); between the positive and negative of photographs, between cinematic motion and static pictures, presence and absence, and even between geographies, host-Canada and mother-land (S. Bertacco). Then, a certain suspension of disbelief is also required to enter the dark/*claire* chamber of a "blur," another keyword that here becomes a common iconic and visual reference that affects memory, photographs, identities and also becomes the Lacanian "stain" that blocks vision of an-other missing gaze, presence, visibility.

"Divided selves" are the subjects of most of the narratives, also filmic ones, here presented: individuals suffering from displacement, caught in their status of un-Canadianness, caught between longing and belonging, for whom it is often necessary to measure themselves against an ancestor. These are only some of the most recurrent textual images and image textualities that emerge in this volume. Finally, an undercurrent of pacifism, born against alienating media-based techno-wars and in favour of a recognition of Otherness (ethnical, racial and sexual – women, Jews, natives) also flows across all the texts analysed by the various contributors to this volume (for example with Ron Bonham). The latter recognition is another typical compulsive feature of Canadian culture besides the recurrent need of, and creative obsession for, image technologies.

This is precisely the reason why Michael Ondaatje's latest novel *Divisadero* (2007) seems to work as the right pre-text to introduce the topic discussed in this volume: image technologies and CanLit. As editors, it is our belief that this attempt at a cross-Atlantic dialogue between scholars of various universities will be regarded as fruitful and productive and it is our hope that this joint research project between the School of Modern Languages and Literatures of the University of Torino, Italy and Vancouver Island University, BC, Canada could be but the first step towards future achievements.

C. C. and R. J. L.

INTRODUCTION

Michael Ondaatje's *Divisadero* and Photography

Carmen CONCILIO

University of Turin, Italy

Of particular relevance here is Michael Ondaatje's latest novel *Divisadero*,[1] and especially the one-and-a-half page chapter called "The Photographs" (187-8) that seems appropriate to introduce the critical and theoretical discussions on image technologies that take different shape in this volume. Certainly Ondaatje's fans and scholars have already jumped to that other chapter called "Photograph" in *Running in the Family* together with the famous ironic picture of Ondaatje's parents enacting "What we think of married life" (1982: 161-3).

To begin with, however, I would like to spend a few words on the novel in general.

Divisadero designs both a precise topography as well as the direction of a destiny: it is the name of a street in San Francisco, and it vaguely hints at distancing.[2] *Divisadero*, as expected, is a very complex narrative, though the plot might appear fairly simple. The story covers a span of time that goes roughly from the 1970s to the years of the Iraq War in 2003, yet there are sideplots rather than subplots that relate to different time periods.

A fit of rage and an explosion of violence push Anna to flee from one of the little settlements of the Californian Gold Rush, setting her to travel first to Paris then to Dému in southern France, where she

1 Michael Ondaatje, *Divisadero* (Toronto: McClelland & Stewart, 2007).

2 "I come from Divisadero Street. Divisadero, from the Spanish word for 'division,' the street that at one time was the dividing line between San Francisco and the fields of the Presidio. Or it might derive from the word *divisar*, meaning 'to gaze at something from a distance.' (There is a 'height' nearby called El Divisadero.) Thus a point from which you can look far into the distance" (2007a: 143).

dedicates her life to composing the biography of the writer Lucien Segura.

The first twist that complicates the narration is immediately evident: Anna, after being the autodiegetic narrator/character in and of the first part of the novel, becomes then the author in/of the second part of the novel. The metamorphosis from character to author, however, is not the only one occurring in the text. Coming of age and migrating to Europe, "The Person Formerly Known as Anna" – as one chapter defines her – has left her past self and life behind and has become a new and different person.

The theme of orphans and quasi-twins is almost obsessive in the novel. Actually, Anna – "The Orphan" as a title recites – is the only legitimate daughter of her father, whose wife died in childbirth, whereas Claire and Coop are later adopted and taken out of compassion to be part of the family. Anna and Claire both lost their mothers: "So there would be two girls, Anna and Claire, born the same week. People assumed that both were his daughters," "As sisters we reflected each other, competed with each other, and our shared idol was Coop" (2007a: 11, 15).

Growing up like sisters, they were almost twins up to the moment the distancing from each other began:

> We were both fifteen years old then, when Coop finally entered the barn and crouched down by me and called me "Claire." So that Claire herself became confused, uncertain for a moment as to who she was. […] We had stepped suddenly into the large uncertain world of adults, and we would now need to be distinctly Anna and distinctly Claire. It became important not to be known as the sister of, or worse, mistaken for, the other (19).

Thus, all the members of the disrupted family develop a new life after Anna's departure. Claire starts working for a lawyer, a public defendant, in spite of her love for horse-riding.[3] Coop becomes a sharper in Vegas and in the nearby towns of Nevada, till his memory is completely erased when beaten into unconsciousness.

The turning point of the novel sounds somewhat similar to Josephine Hart's *Damage*, whose protagonist is named Anna Barton. In *Divisadero*, Anna experiences "a moment of violence that deformed her, all of them. […] it damaged them all, including Claire" (75). In

---

[3] "One fetal twin may absorb the other without malice, and retain in its body a loose relic or two of one of the absorbed twin's femurs. (The living twin grows and becomes an adult; the femur stays fetal.)' That marvel, Annie Dillard, wrote that. And perhaps this is the story of twinship. I have smuggled myself away from who I was, and what I was. But am I the living twin in the story of our family? Or is it Claire? Who is the stilled one?" (2007a: 141).

Damage, Anna warns others: "I have been damaged. Damaged people are dangerous. They know they can survive" (1996: 42). In both cases incest is hinted at, violence erupts and families are destroyed forever. One however might add that most of Ondaatje's characters are damaged individuals. Similarly, New York based Cuban writer Himilce Novas presents in *Mangoes, Bananas and Coconuts* (1996) a plot with father-daughter incest and love between two expatriate twins from Cuba who did not know each other for one had been adopted by a wealthy family, in Miami, while the other had ended up in New York's Spanish Harlem.

Actually, the first part of Ondaatje's novel echoes plots and characters (and images) of his previous works. The impossible love story between Anna and Coop reminds one of the love stories between Buddy Bolden and Robin in *Coming Through Slaughter* (1976). Constant references to jazz pieces and songs – Ondaatje's favourite musical genre – also reinforce this connection.[4] Geniality and recklessness are the main features of Buddy Bolden's life but also of Billy the Kid's, and if not exactly an outlaw, certainly Coop shares many a quality with those predecessors. Particularly, if Bolden ended up mad, Coop ends up with amnesia. With The Kid, then, Coop shares a life on the edge of illegality and almost the same geographical territory, and certainly the same imaginary geography: the Wild West, even though the New Mexico of the 1880s is quite different from the California and Nevada of the 1970s.

More strikingly, the most rehearsed characters are those of Hana and Caravaggio.[5] As happened in *The English Patient* (1992), here too the

4 Jazz is a constant presence in Ondaatje's works, as it is in his most famous novel *The English Patient* and in *Elimination Dance* (1991), his latest short movie.

5 "One afternoon she brought an old gramophone that she had found in the farmhouse, along with some 78s. They wound it up like Model T and danced to 'Begin the Beguine,' wound it up and danced to it again" (*Divisadero* 28).

"A party began in the English patient's room when Caravaggio revealed the gramophone he had found somewhere. I will use to teach you to dance Hana. [...] But this tune, 'How Long Has This Been Going On,' is one of the great songs because the introduction's melody is purer than the song it introduces. And only great jazzmen have acknowledged that" (*The English Patient* 107).

"There was a blue tin jail roof. They were painting the Kingston Penitentiary roof blue up to the sky so that after a while the three men working on it became uncertain of clear boundaries. As if they could climb up further, beyond the tin, into that ocean above the roof. [...] And that was how he escaped [...] Buck and Patrick painted him, covering his hands and boots and hair with blue [...] painted his face blue, so he was gone – to the guards who looked up and saw nothing there" (*In the Skin of a Lion* 179-80).

"Anna went into Rex's Hardware in Petaluma and bought a can of blue paint, a specific blue to match the blue on one of the flags [and blue is sky], and lugged it first love story – between Anna and Coop – is doubled and mirrored by other similar stories. Coop in his "second life" as sharper falls in love with a woman who first reveals herself under her mask of drug addict and only later under her mask of jazz vocalist. In fact, she is a very dangerous kind of mermaid: "she looked like Anna" (2007a: 119). In both love affairs Coop ends up as the passive victim of a fight, and Claire is there to rescue him, though Coop's amnesia makes him assume she is Anna ("Thank you, Anna," 152).

Similarly, on the other side of the Atlantic, Anna is engaged, though in a kind of fatalistic way, in a love story with a gypsy, musician and singer, Raphael. This particular story also echoes another narrative, the film *Chocolat*,[6] where Juliette Binoche – who also acted in the role of Hana in the film *The English Patient*[7] – has a love affair with a gypsy, whose community is ostracized by the villagers of a small rural settlement in the French countryside. Besides, the homophony between the two names Hana and Anna, the openness of the two women to the Other, the foreigner – the Sikh, the Gypsy – the personal movement from North America to Europe of both women in *The English Patient* and *Divisadero*, and their transition from War to Art contribute to creating a bridge between these two novels and the two mentioned films.[8] In *Divisadero*, in particular "the hippie" takes the role Kip plays in *The English Patient* and reacts with sorrow to the radio-news that "Americans were bombing Baghdad" (161). This open critique of war also couples the two novels: the Second World War, the Vietnam War and the neo-imperialistic Gulf Wars are all criticised in this novel.

This intrusion of the two Gulf Wars in the novel also creates a bridge between Ondaatje's work and Daphne Marlatt's *Taken* that has been analysed by Frances Sprout in this volume. Sprout also highlights the complicity and psychological involvement of the spectators with the televised war in Baghdad. This same complicity is hinted at by Ondaatje, though through another medium, that is the radio.

---

uphill to the cabin. Coop brought his table out onto the deck. She eased the top off the can and stirred the paint" (*Divisadero* 30).
"To me [Rafael], for instance, what is most valuable in this room is this blue table" (*Divisadero* 70).

6 *Chocolat*, dir. Lasse Hallstrom, Miramax, USA, 2000.

7 *The English Patient*, dir. Antony Minghella, ed. Walter Murch, Saul Zaentz/Miramax, TigerMoth/Miramax, USA, 1996.

8 Although criticism towards war seems a much less important topic in the film by Minghella. Cf. Gillian Roberts, "'Signs of Omission': *The English Patient*, THE ENGLISH PATIENT, and the Critics," *Essays on Canadian Writing* 76 Spring 2002: 195-215. Glen Lowry, "Between *The English Patients*: Race and the Cultural Politics of Adapting CanLit," *Essays on Canadian Writing* 76 Spring 2002: 216-46.

As a consequence of the doubling of plots and characters, *Divisadero* insists on the presence of doubles. If Coop and Raphael can be paired as outsiders, tightrope walkers living at the margins of other peoples' lives,[9] Raphael's father too, Liébard (not his real name), is a thief by profession and by self-admission. How could one not think of Caravaggio?[10] Besides, he might be considered a mirror image of the writer, Lucien Segura, for "each man regarded the other almost as a mirror" (176). "The Thief" and Segura travel together by horse and cart. The former – accompanied by his second wife, a *Romani*, called Aria (neither her only nor her true name), and by little Raphael – is in search of a location to place their caravan; the latter is in search of a country-house north of Marseille, to find refuge from his former life as a married man. For "the Thief" had also been married, then left his wife after participating in the Second World War where he lost faith in civil life and started roaming the country and living by nature: "He had been journeying up from Italy after the war ended, and had found himself in Belgium [...] he had another wife before the war. [...] There was a chasm for most. There was one life before and one life afterwards. Many decided not to go back to what they had been" (82). Lucien Segura himself "was a poet and later the author of a jeremiad about the Great War" (85).

By now, it should also be clear how collage[11] and different literary/artistic genres find their place in the novel: jazz music, *Casino*-like films, American on-the-road narratives and films, the European picaresque genre, biographical/academic writing are certainly only some of the instances brought up by Ondaatje here. Both in terms of stylistic and linguistic variety, the novel juxtaposes the casino jargon with academic writing, autobiography (first person narratives) and biography (third-person narrative) while using the kind of juxtaposing montage technique that is typical of cinema, to alternate the stories of the various characters.[12] In addition, each reader can pick up his/her own list of echoes and implicit and explicit intertextual references.

---

9 Their most striking affinity is their brown, consumed, and long fingered hands and their firm grip.

10 "There in the darkness he saw Liébard walking along a narrow wall that ran along one side of the inn's garden" (*Divisadero* 177).
"Caravaggio [...] an hour later he is on the roof of the villa" (*The English Patient* 31).

11 "Everything is collage, even genetics. There is the hidden presence of others in us, even those we have known briefly" (2007a: 17).

12 Cf. Bart Testa, "He Did Not Work Here For Long: Michael Ondaatje in the Cinema," *Essays on Canadian Writing* 53 Summer 1994: 154-67.

For instance, after years of academic research, Anna has ended up living in the same house where the writer Lucien Segura had lived. The fact of dwelling in the same house that belonged to the writer she is writing about places Anna in the same position as J. M. Coetzee's Susan Barton, who literally occupied Daniel Defoe's house to write her own version of Robinson Crusoe's adventures. Here Ondaatje, too, seems fascinated by the host and parasite metaphor that widely permeates Coetzee's writings.[13] If in the first part of the novel Coop has behaved as a parasite towards his adoptive father, here Anna too finds herself in a similar position. This act of female colonization of the male sphere – the house and the profession of writer – hides however other, more ethical reasons. Anna has escaped from America, which is now engaged in new imperialistic wars – the Gulf Wars of 1991-2003 – and has reached France to draw in, or be drawn by, its artistic masterpieces. Exactly like Hana before her, who had been mesmerised by the Italian Renaissance frescoes in a small chapel, Anna admires the helicoidal shape of a little church in the village of Barran, and she admits in the novel's prologue that "We have art – Nietzsche said – so that we shall not be destroyed by the truth." The truth being the mere facts of life, one's personal story, or a nation's history.

Art and beauty against war and destruction, I like to think that this is the aesth/ethical message Ondaatje has disseminated in his various texts, as for instance, when he quotes the memorable lines by the Sri Lankan poet Wikkramasinha to uncover the hypocrisy of imperialism:

> Don't talk to me about Matisse.../the European style of 1900, the tradition of the studio/where the nude woman reclines forever/on a sheet of blood//Talk to me instead of the culture generally – /how the murderers were sustained/by the beauty robbed of savages: to our remote/villages the painters came, and our white-washed/mud-huts were splattered with gun fire// (1982: 85).

Another instance is the description of the long ritual ceremony, in *Anil's Ghost*, to restore and paint the destroyed statue of Buddha that lies in the fields where "Buddhism and its values met the harsh political events of the 19th century" (2000: 300).

Finally, the fact that the quotation from Nietzsche had been inspired by Coetzee's speech for the Jerusalem Prize appears as another indirect and tangential homage he pays to the South African Nobel Prize winner.

---

13 Anna's assumption that "no girl has had such an intimacy with a father," referring to the moment when she wished and tried to kill her father, sounds wrong at least in literary terms, for Coetzee's character, Magda, is also on good terms with parricide. Cf. J. M. Coetzee, *In the Heart of the Country* (London: Secker & Warburg, 1977).

Anna's Nietzschean aesthetic statement, though, inscribes her along a genealogy of women writers: firstly, as a successor of Colette's career as a woman-writer. The famous *maudite* and scandalous French writer Anna identifies with in the novel's prologue chose art and writing against life: against her first husband, against what is expected of women, against any pre-packaged truth. Secondly as a successor of her own mother, Lydia Mendez, whose only piece of autobiographic writing – when "women did not write," and "archivists from Berkeley had travelled with tape recorders to capture these lives and the ambience of the past" (2007a: 9) – was recorded in *Interviews with Californios: Women from Early Times to the Present.* Later on, Anna claims she speaks her (ghost)mother's Spanish. Once in France, she relies on "an old map – *La Carte du Tendre Pays* – [...] it was composed by women in an earlier century" (89).

Thus, references to Colette, Jean Genet and Nietzsche, as well as references to Paris and Europe, and also to masks, authorship, identity, anonymity ("For I have taken myself away from who I was with them, and what I used to be. When my name was Anna" – *Prologue* –), all these elements appear in the very first page of the book, and this kind of nomadism identifies not only the female protagonist of the novel, but also all the major and minor characters involved in it.

Particularly, the leitmotif of masks and identity takes the reader to another core-concept in the novel. In *The English Patient*, Count Almásy is fully conscious that Katharine will die because he has the wrong name, a name that sounds foreign and therefore suspicious to the British soldiers whom he asks for help. Anil, the forensic anthropologist who goes back to Sri Lanka to try and discover the truth about the mass murders of the civil war, had bought her name from her brother. In *Divisadero*, Anna speaks of "a 'flock' of Annas" (88); Coop himself has no first name, for Cooper was his surname. Moreover, all the card players, and card sharpers have nicknames, like "the Hippie," or "the Gentile," or even "the Brethren" by which they are known at the tables. Characters like "the Thief" and his wife do not have identifiable and identifying names:

> She is Romani, they have so many names. The secret name, which is never used but is her truest name, which only her mother knows, that's hidden to confuse supernatural spirits it keeps the true identity of the child from them. And the second name, which is a Roma name, is usually used only by them. And that one is Aria.
> And your name, then? Lucien asked.
> I am not Roma, the husband said. [...]
> I cannot call you a thief all the time [...] I need a name.
> Aùguste? Peloque? Liébard? Any of those...

All right, Liébard it is (175-7).
Liébard announced that he was relinquishing the name he'd been using, and was now taking the name Astolphe (182).

Finally, by writing about Lucien Segura, isn't Anna trying to look for what is behind the author's name? Thus she follows an already secure path, that of fictional biography, a genre already experimented with by Ondaatje both with Billy the Kid and with Buddy Bolden. In his so-called "historiographic metafiction," as Linda Hutcheon would name it, "Ondaatje has repeatedly been engaged in an attempt to incorporate marginal figures out of the historical past into a non-historical genre" writes Ajay Heble.[14] Thus characters become aerial beings, nomadic presences, even ghosts, and like the name of the street itself, Divisadero, they hint at movement, distancing, metamorphic voyages. Each character in the novel is on the run from something, particularly a past life, a previous self, a personal or collective war, memories. Parenthetically, it must be said that Ondaatje's interest in ghosts here is hinted at through images of ghost towns that resemble abandoned locations of western movies. While on the run, Anna stops at Colonel Alensworth's abandoned town; the Hippie lives in an old dismissed plane in the no longer functional Jerico Army Base, for the sharpers live an invisible existence to authorities and rivals, while their tricky hands must be invisible to the other card players, as well as to the cameras' eyes that survey the games in the casinos.

"Two Photographs" is the threshold chapter that connects/separates the first part of the novel about Anna, Claire, Coop and their father, as well as about Lucien Segura, the thief, Aria and Raphael, from the second one, or better from the last eighty pages or so, that correspond to the biography of Lucien Segura. In this respect, Ondaatje does not suffer from that resistance to visual culture that the critic Garrett-Petts ascribes to other literati. On the contrary he has always admitted that the starting point of his books were isolated images. In this case, "it was the scene of the horse in the barn. It was almost like being given a photograph in the middle of a story and you have to find all the pictures around it, and then before it and after it."[15] If that was the central image of the book around which a past and a future had to be shaped, the central chapter "Two Photographs" serves the same function.

It must first be stressed how in the novel, too, Ondaatje's vision is translated into photographic images, particularly into framed negatives, where silhouettes dominate:

---

14 Ajay Heble, "Michael Ondaatje and the Problem of History," *Clio* 19.2 1990: 97.

15 Michael Ondaatje, "The fine line between memory and story," *The Irish Times Weekend Review* 29 Sept. 2007: 7.

[He] strolled to the window, opened it and smoked a cigarette there, gazing out, not caring how he looked in that sunlit posture. He would mention later that he was unconcerned with his "silhouette" (73).	Of course she had an arc light in the trunk of the car, and she lifted it out and beamed it towards the strange steeple that rose high into the darkness like a spear. [...] Built in the thirteenth century, the belfry had been constructed like a coil or a screw. It had one of those unexpected, helicoidal shapes – the surface like a helix – so that as it curved up it reflected every compass point of the landscape. We circled the church in the dark (135-6).	He [...] went to the window. There in the darkness he saw Liébard walking along a narrow wall that ran along one side of the inn's garden. There was enough moonlight for Lucien to recognize his travelling companion and this strange act in the middle of the night (177).

In the tradition of light-writing (see Sprout in this volume), these dark shapes against an illumined background, or illumined objects against a dark background suggest an ambiguity in photography as showing presence/absence, reality/ghostly appearance, static moment/movement, the original/the fake, while also hinting at memories in black and white. Unexpectedly, though, the helicoidal architectural shape also becomes the cipher of the novel, for it discloses – like the DNA spiral chain – the complex unroping of family ties:

> It's like a villanelle, this inclination of going back to events in our past, the way the villanelle's form refuses to move forward in linear development, circling instead at those familiar moments of emotion. Only the rereading counts, Nabokov said. [...] We live permanently in the recurrence of our own stories, whatever story we tell (136).

In her new life, Anna, the character who has lost, or has renounced, her name, signs her academic achievements with a new signature, this time renouncing her own authorial and authoritative role. Her new name is a mask, as she admits; her style is borrowed from her sister's journal writing; her Self is hidden behind the life-story of a man who was an orphan (had a stepfather who had been a clockmaker), whose recorded hesitant voice betrayed a ruined love, who all of a sudden abandoned his family disappearing into the countryside.

In the kitchen that Anna now inhabits, there are two photographs pinned up on the wall. One shows an elderly and content Segura coupled by a dark blur: "the only photographic capturing of Lucien's friend Liébard, or Astolphe, who turned on the photographer with a surprising belligerence when he heard the shutter begin to slip into place, turning so quickly that he was able to dissolve his appearance" (188). How can one not think of that much-discussed blank picture of Billy the Kid that opens his/Ondaatje's "real writings" or "left handed poems"?[16] Or of "the Patient" with his burnt out body?[17] The "dark blur," the "white empty frame," the "defaced burnt-out patient" all seem to embody the "aura" Benjamin related to the original, authentic work of art, the legendary, ungraspable quality of those characters, their being linked to a specific time and space so that their unique existence is not transmissible, nor mechanically reproducible. For the aura is tied to the subject's presence.

Similarly, one could speak of the blank photograph of Billy the Kid and of the blurred photograph of Liébard in terms of simulacra. Images that in pretending to portray and fix reality, in "generating models of a real," as Baudrillard would say, end up effacing reality itself: "it is dangerous to unmask images, since they dissimulate the fact that there is nothing behind them," in terms of metaphysical or auratic presence (Baudrillard 1994: 5).

The next picture on the wall is of Anna's naked bust and headdress of greenery. Thus the photographic portrait of the artist/author as an old man (Lucien Segura), with animal-like moustache and a missing tooth, hangs at a small distance from the picture of the artist/biographer as a young lady (the person who used to be Anna), in the pose of a neo-Botticellian spring nymph. Both of them are laughing.

This image faintly echoes the ironic, almost irreverent picture of Ondaatje's own parents in his autobiographical piece of writing, *Running in the Family*, first because of the informality and irony of the pose described, second because of the gender relationships involved. Besides, it also reminds us of Caravaggio's painting *David with the Head of Goliath* in *The English Patient*: "In it, the young warrior holds at the end of his outstretched arm the head of Goliath, ravaged and old. But that is not the true sadness in the picture. It is assumed that the face of David is a portrait of the youthful Caravaggio and the head of Goliath is a portrait of him as an older man" (116). This particular passage has been interpreted by critics as the icon of the young postcolonial

---

16 Cf. Derek Finkle, "From Page to Screen: Michael Ondaatje as Filmmaker," *Essays in Canadian Writing* 53 Summer 1994: 171.

17 "The patient's anonymity, and his (un)readability, make him the perfect blank screen." Stephen Scobie, "The Reading Lesson: Michael Ondaatje and the Patients of Desire," *Essays on Canadian Writing* 53 Summer 1994: 97.

(other)/world killing the old colonial (self)/order.[18] Yet here Self and Other, as well as in *Divisadero*, are just mirror images of the Same. Young David and Old Goliath, represented through young Caravaggio and old Caravaggio, and then young Anna and old Segura, are the two sides of the same authorial function. The *mise en abyme* of the author/artist in his own work of art – Caravaggio's self portrait in his painting, Anna's photo in her biography – re-inscribes a signature there, where it was meant to be erased. The biography becomes auto/author-biography, exactly as it happens in Ondaatje's *Billy the Kid*, where the already mentioned blank opening picture of "the Kid" is coupled by the closing picture of little Michael Ondaatje dressed up as a cowboy.

This is also a device that matches Ondaatje's novel with Leonard Cohen's *coup de theatre* when he involuntarily managed to turn a film biography into a partial autobiography as Keith Harrison shows later in this volume.

Ondaatje himself in his well-known essay "The Silent Partner: Photography in Fiction" admits that almost all his works try to bridge the gap between "the unsaid" even in official historical or family documents and in the only illusionary referential realism of sparse photographs.[19] Yet if words, narratives can fail to convey enough information, photographs might reveal a much more ambiguous nature. Rather than showing reality, they leave space for ghosts. This proves to be true also for most of the essays dealing with photography in this volume, as in the cases of Daphne Marlatt, Michael Ondaatje and Stan Douglas.

Going back for a moment to Liébard's missing image, in this case too, Ondaatje is touching on a widely used metaphor in postcolonial writings. Liébard managed to trick the photographer and his shutter so as to become invisible, or at least indistinguishable and unidentifiable, similarly the legendary Billy the Kid managed not even to impress the film. So that the experimental photographer trying to capture "a picture

---

18 "[It] can be seen as an image of the postcolonial world and its texts holding the imperial world and its texts at arm's length in an unresolved tension of kinship and impatience of 'fury and fascination.' [It] suggests an emergent postcolonial subject and the embodiment of a burnt-out imperial discourse in all its complexity. The text of the young Indian and the 'Englishman' are in some ways inverse reflections of each other, in other ways carbon copies." Johan U. Jacobs, "Michael Ondaatje's *The English Patient* (1992) and Postcolonial Impatience," *JLS/TWL* June/Junie 1997: 107.

19 "That is especially what I am drawn to, especially the unspoken and unwritten stories – the 'un-historical' stories." Michael Ondaatje, interview with Linda Hutcheon, Linda Hutcheon, and Marion Richmond (eds.), *Other Solitudes: Canadian Multicultural Fictions* (Toronto: Oxford UP, 1990): 198.

of Billy made with the Perry shutter as quick as it can be worked" (1970a: 5), remains with an empty frame. Both "the Thief" and "the Kid" once photographed become ghosts. Literally, as Susan Sontag suggests, photography has killed them by trying to immortalize them, by trying to transform them from subjects into objects.[20] As for Roland Barthes, he speaks of the *Spectrum* in photography, that is "that vaguely frightening thing that is present in any photograph: the return of the dead" (2000: 9). Yet, in *Divisadero*, it is not only the photo in itself that makes the ghost manifest, it is also what remains outside the frame that becomes ghostly. The surfacing ghost/blur of the father figure (Liébard) here is mirrored by the ghost of the son/photographer (Rafael), for he is missing from the picture, too: "We look at this picture and imagine also the person with the camera, walking backwards at the same pace as the subject so that she remains in focus. [...] the unseen photographer" (188). Incidentally, Rafael is the *operator* in Barthes's terms in both cases, for he took the picture of Segura with his own (blurred) father and years later he takes the picture of Anna.

So, while theorization on photography (Barthes, Sontag) stresses the reification of the subject, that is the person-becoming-ghost, writers who have experienced migration, uprooting and "translation" into other cultures seem to further complicate the argument.

The photographer is a recurrent figure in Ondaatje's works and consequently elaborations on light writing are frequent, too: the anonymous photographer in *Billy the Kid*, for instance, experiments in the way Eadweard Muybridge was doing with horses in motion. In Coming Through Slaughter, apart from the Dolphins' sonograph which represents another kind of light writing about sounds waves, Bellocq, "a crip that Buddy knew who photographed whores" (1976: 50), destroys the only one picture of Bolden "taking him out of the company. Then he dropped the negative into the acid tray and watched it bleach out to grey" (53), "the original" is thus destroyed preventing simulacra, copies, to be reproduced out of it, as if "the real" was an inimitable work of art in itself; besides, Bellocq disfigures, beheads and cuts the pictures of the whores he had previously collected, damaging and mutilating their bodies perhaps in answer to his own physical deformity. Like with the God Shiva, or simply as an artist, creation and destruction are in his power.

In *The English Patient*, Clifton is an aerial photographer, and Caravaggio, the thief and spy, had been betrayed by the photographs

20 "It turns people into objects," "A photograph is both a pseudo-presence and a token of absence." Susan Sontag, *On Photography* (Harmondsworth: Penguin, 1977): 14, 16.

taken by a woman at a party during the war: "one of the women had brought a camera and was snapping at the German officers, and I was caught in mid-step, walking across the ballroom. In mid-step, the beginning of the shutter's noise making me jerk my head towards it" (35). The interesting thing here is that Caravaggio slips into the woman's room in order to steal her camera. The room is in complete darkness and Caravaggio is completely naked – not to leave any print and to avoid making any noise – only his body is caught by the lights of a passing car. And he interprets the scene for the reader as follows: "The story he told someone's child years ago about the person who searched for his shadow – as he is now looking for this image of himself on a piece of film" (38).

In this case light writing is interpreted literally as a body lit/written up, individuated, shaped by light and nakedness, a white body out of a dark room/chamber that has lost its shadow. Significantly too, the photographer who has accidentally captured Caravaggio's image is the indirect and probably unwilling cause of the incident that mutilates his body: his thumbs are cut less as a punishment for his thieving and more to exort pieces of news from him by the Italian Intelligence.

In *Divisadero*, Liébard shares with Caravaggio the comprehensible hate a thief feels towards cameras. Thus it is his son, Raphael, who becomes a photographer.

The ghostly absence of the photographer that has been discussed so far is also a trait Coetzee explores in *Age of Iron*:

> We were photographed that day in a garden. [...] I recognize the place. [...] Who are the ghosts, who the presences? Who outside the picture, leaning [...] against the edge of the rectangle, bending it, bursting it in? *Dies irae, dies illa* when the absent shall be present and the present absent. No longer does the picture show who were in the garden frame that day, but who were not there. [...] The fixing did not hold or the developing went further than one would ever have dreamed – who can know how it happened? But they have become negatives again, a new kind of negative in which we begin to see what used to lie outside the frame, occulted.[21]

Here the absent photographer is most probably the black gardener, who because of apartheid is even invisible to history.

Also Salman Rushdie speaks about "outsideness" as a new category: "The only people who see the whole picture [...] are the ones who step

---

[21] J.M. Coetzee, *Age of Iron* (Vintage: New York, 1991): 111-2. Cf. also Carmen Concilio, "'Worthy of the world': The Narrator/Photographer in Salman Rushdie's *The Ground Beneath Her Feet*," Elsa Linguanti, and Viktoria Tchernichova (eds.), *The Great Work of Making Real. Salman Rushdie's* The Ground Beneath Her Feet (Pisa: ETS, 2003): 117-27.

out of the frame."[22] Besides, in the same context, he also mentions subjects who have been completely erased from the picture or who only appear as a half figure in it, and finally the narrator/photographer turns to take pictures of ghost-farms. Therefore, from complete outsiders to the image, to completely empty frames, to blurred stains, to half portraits, to full portraits, photography becomes the site for considerations on identity, legitimacy, anonymity and (legendary) ghosts. So if it were possible to claim that there is a peculiar stance in the postcolonial, or in the diasporic global novel, it lies in the disempowerment of the photographer, who no longer seems to occupy that privileged position of the voyeur, the shooting eye/I, being forever outside the picture, invisible, and often producing unreliable re-productions.

Why does Ondaatje interrogate himself and in the meanwhile pose questions about orphans, twins, lost mothers and fathers, name-changes, outsiders, ghosts, wars of the West, in a novel that does not aspire primarily to sociological engagement and touches political matters only tangentially? "She was hearing about America bombing a civilian city. [...] We are the barbarians too. We keep letting this happen" (*Divisadero* 162).

The answer is the key to Ondaatje's works as a whole, and therefore not easy to provide as all-comprehensive. All his texts actually touch upon some – if not all – of these issues, which are complicated by the role played by history and (loss of) memory. And it is not to avoid answering that I would like to summarise something the Indian novelist Amitav Ghosh writes about "diasporic" writers like Michael Ondaatje.[23] When they write about what they have lost, or what they have left behind, their homelands/mother-lands, they write elegies of homecoming with the voice of orphans not only of an almost-mother, but of History itself. And Anna claims: "Those who have an orphan's sense of history love history. And my voice has become that of an orphan" (141). They write in the mood of a lamentation, says Ghosh, for the loss of a Paradise. And many immigrants do not write about their arrival in the new world, but rather of their departure from the old world. It is as if they reached their future, the host country, through looking back to their past, the lost paradise of their homelands and of their childhood. Diaspora is different from an Exodus. Being a diasporic writer involves this backward gaze to the Paradise lost, whereas the exodus experience implies looking forward to the Promised Land.

[22] Salman Rushdie, *The Ground Beneath Her Feet* (London: Jonathan Cape, 1999): 42-3.

[23] Amitav Ghosh, *Incendiary Circumstances. Chronicle of the Turmoil of Our Time* (New York: Houghton Miffin, 2007).

If Ondaatje's novel shows such a sensitivity towards themes of loss (of parents, love, languages and names), towards outsiders, otherness and people lost to history ("I am a person who discovers archival subtexts in history and art," 137), towards failures in photography as a bridge to the past and to other people's lives it is to be related to his own experience of migrant, diasporic subject.

Gotraskhalana is a term in Sanskrit poetics for calling a loved one by a wrong name, and means literally "stumbling on the name." That word is the title of a chapter in the novel, though this reference to Sanskrit is exactly this looking back to a lost past, a lost culture, a lost love, a lost language. The simple, little linguistic slip/lapsus that points back to Sri Lanka provides the key to my previous question:

> The last Sinhala word I lost
> was *vatura*. The word for water.
> Forest water. The water in a kiss. The tears
> I gave to my ayah Rosalin on leaving
> the first home of my life.
> […]
> No photograph of her, no meeting
> since the age of eleven,
> not even knowledge of her grave.
> Who abandoned who, I wonder now.[24]

Memory has a fundamental role both in this poem, the one chosen by Ghosh to epitomize exile, and in the novel: "*Divisadero*, more than any of my other books, looks at how memory governs us,"[25] Ondaatje admits. The damage done by a loss, by the breaking of family bonds, by losing a language while writing in another language, from another continent, becoming another one-self, these are all recurrent themes that are at stake in Ondaatje's *œuvre*, and also in *Divisadero*. Thus, it is surprisingly reassuring – if proof be needed – to find the poem *One Art*, about the art of losing, by Elizabeth Bishop entirely dedicated to loss, lost objects, lost cities and people loved, quoted in its first and final drafts right in the middle of Ondaatje's *Conversations* about the art of editing film, the need to cut and take away and eliminate things.[26]

A final consideration is to be dedicated to those disturbing/fascinating minor themes that permeate Ondaatje's poetics: violence and

---

24 Michael Ondaatje, *Handwriting* (New York: Alfred A. Knopf, 1999): 50.

25 Michael Ondaatje, "The fine line between memory and story," *op. cit.*, 7.

26 Michael Ondaatje, *The Conversations. Walter Murch and the art of editing film* (Toronto: Vintage Canada, 2002): 138-9.

animals. A dog is also present in this novel, and violent acts against animals are hinted at here and there as in many of his works.[27] The suspicion I sensed at first, when tentatively embedding references to J. M. Coetzee's works, that his books have become a favourite reading for Ondaatje, has been confirmed in a recent interview:

> At the end of the interview, when asked if there is anything else he'd like to say, Ondaatje says yes. What he comes out with is a surprise, a non-sequitur. "I've been thinking about animal life the last few days," he says slowly. "Coetzee [the South African-born novelist] talks about this, and obviously he's very obsessive about this. I think the whole respect of animals as much as humans is a very interesting thing. And landscape. The wideness of it is much greater than we think when we are as kids or teenagers. That's what I've been mulling over lately, the affection one has for certain trees or certain animals." Given this, does he have a dog? He does. "Stella. She is a brown hound. Partly mongrel." Then he laughs. "But of course!" Only a couple of minutes earlier he's been talking about how he loves the "mongrel form" of fiction; fiction that is rich with a mix of styles and forms. A mongrel.[28]

And this is also a recurrent refrain in Ondaatje's interviews: "We are all mongrels."

Mongrel art forms seem to take shape polyphonically also in the present volume, starting from Lucia Boldrini's exploration of "anamorphosis and photography" in Michael Ondaatje's *The Collected Works of Billy the Kid*, where pictures reproduce only slant and slight relationships with their sources, transforming them and re-signifying them through various degrees of slippage, rather than simply reproducing them. Moving then to Jeffrey Orr's conceptualization of "intersemiotic translation," he examines translation between two different media, in Ondaatje's shifting of texts/photography, with relevance given to the body, text, language and desire.

Blended genres, undecidable selves, photographic and cinematic techniques bridge the writing on Ondaatje with the other writers tackled in the present volume. Taking Ondaatje as a point of departure, the present volume assumes as an implicit theoretical background recent advances in postcolonial and postmodern theory; but the critics herein also engage in a wider, post-theory approach, one that returns to key philosophers and theorists of film and photography, such as Roland Barthes, Walter Benjamin and Susan Sontag. Such an engagement suggests a desire for a dialogic, post-theory reading of traditional image

---

[27] Derek Finale, *op. cit.*

[28] Michael Ondaatje, "The fine line between memory and story," *op. cit.*, 7.

technologies in Canadian literature, and thus the further resonances with the theories of Mikhail Bakhtin.

Frances Sprout scrutinises Daphne Marlatt's *Taken*, where writing becomes a sort of photo-*graphein* itself by means of structural and stylistic references to the photochemical process, as the play between light and dark, the continuum of positive and negative, vegetation as a version of light-writing, and beyond the frame ghosts. Simona Bertacco explores the pairing of Marlatt's *Steveston* and of Robert Kroetsch's *The Ledger* as texts made up of a verbal/visual materiality that calls into action the reader as if he or she were the visitor of an art gallery and the author as depository of visual, verbal and oral forms of discourse and as collector of palimpsests made up of documentary material and the vernacular voice of storytelling of the traditional long poem. Besides the poems, Bertacco salvages the often underestimated presence of the photographic and visual elements in Marlatt's work, which is the fruit of her collaboration with the photographer Robert Minden.

Similarly, Richard Lane presents the works of Joseph Dandurand and Stan Douglas, two richly eclectic artists whose "revolutionary images *cross* and at times *disrupt* theoretical domains, or, more accurately speaking, are complex constellations." Poetry and image, or the poetry of the image itself also in this case are joined by necessity of – in Benjamin's words – the "dialectical image," that is not only the dialectic between poem (present) and photograph (past) but the short circuit that each textuality/visuality *per sé* enacts and then together they function as postcolonial and as aboriginal subversive discourse.

Further, the film *Mr Leonard Cohen*, which is the object of Keith Harrison's study, epitomises the slippage and reversal of a film biography into a partial autobiography due to Cohen's acting and self-representation. By framing a photograph of his grandfather within the lens of the movie camera, the young poet/singer/writer identifies with his older ancestor, a poet himself, thus showing "intergenerational images of the self and enquiring into how identities are composed, transferred and recomposed." By doing so, Cohen "almost usurped the directors, and staged himself for the lens with wit and grace," as Anna does with Segura/Ondaatje's biography.

Between Marlatt's literal light-writing and Cohen's performative mode, Ron Bonham's analysis of Anne Marie MacDonald's *Fall on your Knees* also presents a writing that becomes movie-like because of the use of point of view, reality in movement, photography, the technique of rhythmic montage. Also the language and metalanguage in the novel become explicit references to filmmaking, so that the gaze, framing, shooting, seeing and witnessing become crucial agencies as proper to image technologies.

CHAPTER 1

The Anamorphosis of Photography in Michael Ondaatje's *The Collected Works of Billy the Kid*

Lucia BOLDRINI

Goldsmiths College, London

Made up of poetry, prose, photographs, drawings, (edited) citations, empty or partially filled frames, Michael Ondaatje's *The Collected Works of Billy the Kid: Left-Handed Poems*[1] is a notoriously difficult book to describe, or to ascribe to a particular genre. The mixture of texts in the first and third person, spoken by Billy or about Billy, and of biographical accounts locates it on the boundary between (fictional) autobiography, biography, and poetic reconstruction; the use of photographs draws attention to its (supposedly) documentary nature, while the use of drawings and the reproduction of the cover of a volume of the Five Cents Wide Awake Library suggest otherwise. The empty frame that appears on page 5 of *The Collected Works*, over the caption that starts "*I send you a picture of Billy* […]," immediately tells us that "capturing" the elusive Billy, the "Wanted" outlaw is impossible: it may be our task as readers to try to fill the empty frame, but we shall have to accept that no tangible "Reward" will be paid to us, that the frame will remain white, and that we may be able to fill it only partially by inserting other subjectivities into the frame – the author/editor's (Ondaatje defines himself as "editor," rather than "author," in the "Credits," 1970b: 109), or perhaps our own: at the end of the book a photograph of a young Michael Ondaatje appears within a large and otherwise empty frame (107), and we may feel tempted, even encouraged, to add ours as we read of and fill in, with our own experiences and memories of Western myths, the character of Billy. Billy himself may prove elusive, yet if we invest some time and effort in the hunt, and in particular in studying the photographs (including the

1 Toronto: House of Anansi, 1970.

framed white square), we may indeed achieve some reward, and discover a different story from the one that these images appear to convey. While they do not document Billy (his appearance, his deeds, his life, his surrounds), the photographs nevertheless document something that turns out to be also relevant to the frontier life of which Billy was such a notorious protagonist, and whose myths have shaped, and continue to shape, the imagination not only of Americans but of generations of individuals around the world. Asked when his interest in the character of Billy began, Ondaatje remarked:

> From about the age of seven. Roughly when the last picture in the book (of me in Ceylon in a cowboy outfit) was taken. Then it wasn't specifically Billy the Kid, but *cowboys* that was important. So around 1967 when I began the book the cowboy had germinated. The question that's so often asked – about why I wrote about an American hero – doesn't really interest me cos I hardly knew what an American was when the image of "cowboy" began that germinating process. I was writing about something that had always interested me, something within myself, not out there in a specific country or having some political or sociological meaning. I'm not interested in politics on that public level. The recent fashion of drawing journalistic morals out of literature is I think done by people who don't love literature or who are not capable of allowing its full scope to be seen (qtd. in Mundwiler 1984: 12-3).[2]

While Ondaatje thus refuses to authorize an explicitly political, postcolonial interpretation of his book or his choice of Billy as the "hero" of the text (Mukherjee 1994: esp. 96-132),[3] his words do not necessarily deny that such meanings exist in literature: it is "journalistic morals" that Ondaatje rejects, not the "full scope" and complexity of literature – and this may include a reflection on the appeal of certain myths, and on the way certain images and identifications operate. It is hard to believe that Ondaatje would have been oblivious to the fact that the "cowboy" that so fascinated him and millions of other children round the globe is part of a dominant culture whose cultural imperialism the seven year old Michael may have been innocent of, but whose manner of transmitting ideologies the grown up Sinhalese-Canadian writer must have recognized. Whether he meant to "have a go at" the ideologies that sustain the diffusion of American legends is beside the point. The impression was left, and any later "germination" of Billy or the figure of the cowboy is a reaction to that initial impression, to the way cultural imperialism turns its subjects into willing co-operators.

2 From an interview in *Manna* 1, March 1972, 20.

3 And for this rejection of "politics on that public level" Ondaatje has been castigated by some post-colonial critics.

Ondaatje's unconventional, obscure, decentred, disturbing presentation of Billy is in its own way a political response – through the "full scope" of the complex medium of literature (a complexity that also involves the use and manipulation of images and their referents) – to the imposition of a simple figure of identification, that is to say, to the manner in which hegemonic ideologies work. It is essential therefore to acknowledge that while this book, as has been forcefully argued, does construct Billy as a verbal and visual text that has no clear recoverable referent outside its own textuality (cf. Kamboureli 1988: 115-29; Jones 1989: 26-38), at the same time it cannot be read simply as empty postmodern play that posits reference as a "problem" by foregrounding its own metafictionality and that of the documents to which it refers within a never ending chain of discursivity. The ideological dimension, like the historical, the auto/biographical, and the documentary (referential), remains central to the book and needs to be confronted. As Ondaatje stated in a later interview, "Ideally, I want that mental landscape and the personal story to wrestle against the documentary. I think the documentary element is so essential to our lives that to ignore it in the novel is a problem" (Bush 1994: 243).

Earlier I said that the photographs in *The Collected Works* also demand to be interpreted, that investing some time and effort into their origins and historical referents may eventually pay off. Let me take the "empty" frame as a paradoxical example. A clue to what it may contain is offered by Billy's memory of the famous photograph taken by a "travelling photographer" in 1880, of which Paulita Maxwell claims: "I don't think it does Billy justice" (Ondaatje 1970b: 19; the photograph does not appear in the book). Billy says: "I remember, when they took the picture of me there was a white block down the fountain road where somebody had come out of a building and got off the porch onto his horse and ridden away while I was waiting standing still for the acid in the camera to dry firm" (68). The "white block" that appears in the photograph is not an object registered on the plate but movement that did not register, as the shutter had to stay open long enough to allow the chemicals to fix the image, but too long to be able to capture and record the man riding off. This may bring to mind the first known daguerrotype, *View of the Boulevard du Temple* (1839), which recorded in clear, sharp detail the view of the street; though the scene should have been crowded, however, the only human figures we can see are a man having his boots blackened and the boot-black, the only ones who remained in the same position long enough for their image to fix on the plate. The rest of the street is eerily empty, apparently lifeless, as life went about its business, not stilled (Frizot 1998: 28).[4] Thus the square on page 5 is indeed "empty," showing us nothing; but its whiteness may also signal too much life, Billy's refusal to lie still even after his death, to let his legend fix into History. The "caption" beneath it also helps us place the image at a particular moment of the history of photography, a phase that emphasised the documentary potential of the technique while raising new challenges for the realist impulse that drove it. These are the aspects that I wish to explore further in this essay by looking at the photographs reproduced in *The Collected Works of Billy the Kid*, their sources, their transformations and their re-signification.

In the "Credits" at the end of the book, Ondaatje lists a number of original sources that he has "edited, rephrased, and slightly reworked" (these borrowings are clearly identified in the text by the italic type). As has been pointed out (Kamboureli 1988: 116; Barbour 1993: 43), while the citations are essentially faithful to the original, their extraction from the original context and their re-location to a new one inevitably re-orient their meaning and their force. Let us take again the "caption" under the "empty" frame on page 5. In the "Credits," Ondaatje acknowledges the role of the frontier photographer L. A. Huffman as his source: "The comment about taking photographs around 1870-1880 is by the great Western photographer L. A. Huffman and appears in his book *Huffman, Frontier Photographer*. (Some of the photographs in this book are his.)" But, as Douglas Barbour has pointed out, no such book by Huffman, or with such a title, exists. The words come instead from the chapter "L. A. Huffman, Frontier Photographer," in Mark H. Brown and W. R. Felton, *The Frontier Years: L. A. Huffman, Photographer of the Plains* (New York: Henry Holt & Co., 1955), and are taken from two different letters sent by Huffman to his father and discussing his photographic techniques, the first of which starts "I send you a picture of Bessie" – Bessie being Huffman's five months old daughter (Barbour 1993: 43, 222, No. 16). As Barbour remarks, "Once it was an uncomplicated commonsensical piece of writing, the pronouns neatly fixed, but now that it is cited it is also re-sited, slipping its moorings in history, that supposed guarantor of 'reality,' to float into the ocean of fiction, where it can never again be anchored in apparent referentiality. In its original text, the pronouns were specific, but now, on the first page of this new text, commenting on a photo that does not

4 Of the daguerrotype, Samuel F.B. Morse wrote: "Moving objects leave no impression. The boulevard, though constantly crossed by a flood of pedestrians and carriages, appeared completely deserted, apart from a person who was having his boots polished. His feet must, of course, have remained immobile for a certain time, one of them being placed on the boot-black's box, the other on the ground." Qtd. in Michel Frizot, "1839-1840. Photographic Developments."

exist, and speaking for a nonreferential 'I' to an equally nonreferential 'you,' it expands into a multiplicity of possible meanings." This, as Barbour concludes, effects from the start "A slippery rhetorical linkage of logos, topos and ethos [that] will hold throughout the rest of the book" (1993: 43). The photographs reproduced in *The Collected Works* respond to the same logic; they too are citations whose redeployment and "slight" editing re-signifies them, and puts the text into a dialogue with the sources from which they have been excerpted.

A similar kind of slippage also occurs on pages 30 and 31, where Sallie is first introduced through words excerpted from Walter Noble Burns's *The Saga of Billy the Kid* (1926; acknowledged in the "Credits"): "(*Miss Sallie Chisum, later Mrs Roberts, was living in Roswell in 1924, a sweet faced, kindly old lady of a thousand memories of frontier days*)" (Ondaatje 1970b: 30). The sentence is placed in brackets at the top of the page, set off from Sallie's own words about her house (also taken from Burns) on the bottom half of the page. The layout makes the words in brackets *look like* a caption for the facing photograph on page 31. The impression left by this image is undoubtedly that of a photograph of the time: its quality is similar to that of the other photographs attributed to Huffman, it convinces us of its age, and conveys a sense of the old West; however, it is anything but a photograph of an "old lady." In fact, it is a photograph taken by Michael Ondaatje of his friends Stuart and Sally Mackinnon, to whom the book is dedicated (Jewinski 1994: 67). One may wonder whether Ondaatje's choice was affected by the coincidence of Sally's and Sallie's names. One may also wonder whether deputy Mackinnon (Ondaatje 1970b: 92), whose name, as far as I have been able to ascertain, does not appear in any of the historical accounts of Billy's final capture, might be another of Ondaatje's silent jokes – like the naming of the mad breeder of dogs after another friend and dedicatee of the book, Ken Livingstone. Whatever innocent fun Ondaatje may be having at our (or his friends') expense, placing Burns's introduction of "Miss Chisum" next to the photograph of a couple dressed as frontier settlers creates a powerful reality effect and raises the issue of authenticity as a sense, an impression, perhaps an *emotion* (Ondaatje 1970b: 109), rather than a fact-based certainty. To say it with Roland Barthes, the power of photography is that it conveys the strongest sense that something has really been, has existed; of an essential, noemic "*Ça-a-été*," "That-has-been" (Barthes 1980: 120-1 *passim*; 2000: 76-7 *passim*). This is not another example of the camera lying as it does in the case of Billy's photograph according to Paulita ("I don't think it does Billy justice"): it is the manipulation of the material and its juxtaposition with the text that deceive us. There is no doubt that "*Ça-a-été*"; what remains uncertain is the deixis of this "*Ça*." What is called into question is the relationship between text and image, and this has an important retrospective effect: if text and image are not related here on pages 30 and 31, though they appear to be, they may not be related elsewhere either: why should the Huffman quotation on page 5 function as a caption for the empty frame above it and not, as I shall suggest later, (also) for the photograph on the front cover, the only photo we have seen so far? And why should that frame represent Billy at all, and not, for example, as I shall also suggest later, the *tabula rasa* that we must make of our minds and preconceptions before coming to this book?

Let us therefore turn to "the great Western photographer L. A. Huffman," "his book *Huffman, Frontier Photographer*," and in particular his photographs and their *editing* in order to investigate how Ondaatje's inaccurate attribution in the "Credits" may serve as a pointer to other similar inaccuracies, or instances of not so "slight reworking."[5]

Brown and Felton's *The Frontier Years* describes Laton Alton Huffman's life and work, and reproduces many of his photographs. Descendant of frontiersmen in Ohio and Virginia, sometimes referred to as "kid" (1955: 52, 79), Huffman continued to pursue the frontier as it moved west, as photographer but also as cattle ranger and as hunter, mainly of buffaloes. These activities he also photographed, as well as Indians, soldiers, and landscapes whose beauty he extolled. He sent many letters to his father describing the challenges for a pioneer photographer, especially with slow shutters, slow films, and the uneven quality of materials. "The problem of stopping motion," Brown and Felton explain, "was one with which Huffman apparently did considerable experimenting," and quote from three letters of 1885, the first two of which, as we have seen, contain the words that Ondaatje uses, almost verbatim though compressing them into a single paragraph, under the empty frame on the opening page (1955: 43). Brown and Felton also remark:

> The lack of definition, sometimes called fuzziness, which may be noted at the edges of some of the pictures was caused by using the widest possible lens opening. This, of course, was necessary because of the 'instantaneous' shutter speed, and the slowness of the film. That he shot from horseback is obvious when the perspective is noted [...] (43).

5 Photography as a theme has been discussed by most critics that have written on *The Collected Works of Billy the Kid* (e.g. Nodelman 1980: 68-79; MacLulich 1981: 107-19). Little has been written on the photographs themselves, except perhaps by Monica Turci, *Approaching that Perfect Edge*, esp. the section "The Ambiguity of the Photograph: Texts and Images in *The Collected Works of Billy the Kid*" (2001: 36-48).

Five photographs in *The Collected Works of Billy the Kid* (13, 23, 45, 59, 91) come from *The Frontier Years*, though only one comes from the chapter "L. A. Huffman. Frontier Photographer," the title referenced in the "Credits." This is the photo reproduced on page 23 of *The Collected Works*, printed on page 34 of Brown and Felton (photo 11), and called "Ye Studio-La Atelier 18 x 40. 3 rooms." A note explains that this was Huffman's studio at Fort Keogh (Huffman applied to be post photographer there in 1878). Brown and Felton also add: "The type of construction was similar to that used in the cantonment except that many of the roofs at the first post were flat. Note the double window at the right and the skylight" (252).[6] The reproduction of this photograph in the original House of Anansi edition of *The Collected Works* has worse definition than that in Brown and Felton; the quality of the reproduction in later editions and translations is worse still. The sky over the roof of the building seems divided horizontally in two, the lower area of a darker grey than the higher, so that it appears as though we were looking over distant misty hills. No such impression is given by the photograph in *The Frontier Years*. Because of the blurriness, the window on the right is hardly visible in late editions of *The Collected Works of Billy the Kid*, and it could be missed even in the Anansi edition.

No clear relation can be identified between the photograph and the context in which it appears in *The Collected Works*. It is placed after the description of the shooting of Charlie Bowdre at Tivan Arroyo, and we might think this is the house in which Billy and his friends came under fire. But the passage concludes, "No windows, the door open so we could see. Four horses outside" (Ondaatje 1970b: 22): certainly not a description in which we would recognise the building in the photograph. The length of the construction – about double its width – might suggest that this is the barn ("twenty yards long, about ten yards wide," 17), where Billy rests during a fever only a few pages earlier, in an episode that ends with the drunken rats eating one another and Billy shooting them all. But the three people chatting amiably outside (a woman, sitting, and two men, standing) hardly support such identification. Small groups of people – usually two men and a woman: Billy, John and Sallie Chisum – are in the habit of chatting for hours at the Chisums' ranch, but the building in the photograph has none of the characteristics of their house, such as the porch where they spend their evenings. Thus the scarce clarity of the image extends to its link to the verbal text: fuzzy, unclear, difficult to pin down. The same is true of the other photographs.

---

6 Note to photo 11.

The photos on pages 45 and 59 (the one on page 91 is a detail of the former) are taken from chapter 3 of *The Frontier Years*, "Hide-Hunters and Sportsmen," which describes the buffalo hunts. Buffaloes were usually hunted for hide, in stands in which up to 100 animals (sometimes even more) could be killed; as Brown and Felton explain, often the hunters did not bother to cure the meat, abandoning it on the plains. Wolf hunting too frequently consisted in mass killing of animals, and many wolfers travelled with a pack horse outfit, but some used instead a little cart to carry their equipment (1955: 73, 80); it is a detail from one such wolfer's cart that appears in the image on page 59 of *The Collected Works*, taken from Huffman's photograph "Wolfer's two-wheeled outfit used in rough country," printed on page 80 (photo 32) of *The Frontier Years*. As in the previous case, the photo in Brown and Felton is sharper and clearer than in its reproductions in *The Collected Works*, especially the later editions. The detail excerpted by Ondaatje only shows man and dog; from the position of the man and the bundles and dog behind him we make out that they are travelling on a cart (we just discern the reins in his hands), but we see no details of the cart itself, or the horses. The original photograph shows however that the horses are not moving: the impression of movement is the result of the cropping of the image.

Again, the relationship between the photo and the text is not clear. In the poem on the previous page (Ondaatje 1970b: 58), Billy is catching flies with his left hand[7] – surely a hunting of sorts, but not of the sort evoked by the photograph. The prose text printed below the image suggests a more immediate possible referent for the dog in the photograph: Henry, the bassett the Chisums had had imported from England "by ship, then train, then Sallie had met the train and brought it the last seventy miles in a coach" (59). The wrong dog (the one in the picture is clearly not a bassett) and the wrong means of transport (a cart, not a coach): but still a dog on a horse-drawn vehicle. Another loose link may be found in the fact that the photograph represents a wolf hunter, and bassets were bred for hunting. The wrong type of hunting, though: bassets, according to Sallie's explanation, were bred for fat noblemen who could not keep up with faster hounds. This is the cue for John Chisum to tell the story of another instance of grotesque dog breeding that ends in appalling violence; similarly, Huffman's photographs of wolfers are contextualised by Brown and Felton through stories of grotesque mass killing of wolves with strychnine (carcasses of killed buffaloes were stuffed with strychnine crystals and left out to

[7] At least, we infer the speaker is Billy, from the birthday on November 23 and the swiftness of the left hand; however, the references to "neon," not invented until 1910 in France, may raise some doubts.

attract wolves; if the bait was frozen, it would yield 10 to 50 wolves, who would also freeze as they died; wolfers would then have to wait until they defrosted, sometimes until the spring, before skinning them, 1955: 79-80).

The picture on page 45 of *The Collected Works* is the wolfer's cabin reproduced on page 88 of *Frontier Years* (photograph No. 38). Again, the print in Brown and Felton has better definition and contrast, showing in much clearer detail objects such as the gun holster hanging from the wall; the stove; the pots hanging on the right. The top left and right corners are darker but not as murky as in Ondaatje's reproduction. The photo in *Frontier Years* transmits detail, relief, depth and volume, and gives the sense of a tidy, clean, basic but well kept cabin; in the Anansi edition of *The Collected Works* the cabin also appears tidy, but the lack of contrast flattens it out; in later editions it looks oppressive, almost sooty. The original clearly shows a source of light on the right, over the table; its presence can be surmised in the reproduction that appears in the Anansi edition, but is not at all clear in later ones. It is not until a blown up detail from this photograph is presented again on page 91 that we clearly distinguish the gun holster with all its bullets, the rifle against the bed, the jacket on the left, and what looks like a flask hanging from the wall. Brown and Felton quote Huffman's own note to this photo:

> A professional wolfer's 'roost' in the Hell Creek Breaks of Northern Montana. Wolfers led a lonely life. Some of them are educated men and tidy house-keepers. A wolfer destroys wolves for the bounty paid by the state, the pelts sold to fur dealers, and ofttimes for an additional fee from nearby cattlemen.' L.A.H. (Sieber's cabin) (1955: 254).[8]

Huffman's suggestion of hunting for bounty may bring to mind the professional bounty killers of traditional Wild West stories going after "Wanted" men – men like Billy, but once again there is no clear link between image and text in *The Collected Works.* Just before encountering the picture on page 45 we witness Billy determinedly hunting and killing a sick cat (Ondaatje 1970b: 44-5) – a slim link indeed with the wolfers' hunts. If we seek a bed and a gun in the text, two episodes in particular stand out. About halfway between the photograph of the cabin and the reprint of the detail, Billy, scanning his room as he wakes up at the Chisums' after a night of heavy drinking, sees Angela still asleep, while "on the nail above the bed the black holster and gun is coiled like a snake, glinting also in the early morning white" (71). The association is tempting, but the holster and gun in this photograph is neither coiled like a snake nor does it seem to glint in the early morning white, and there is no Angela on the bed. Wrong bed,

8 Note to photo 38.

wrong holster, wrong gun. On page 90, just before the detail of the photograph is reprinted, Billy hears the hum of flies (we have already seen Billy catching flies in his fist in proximity to another photograph), the crackling noises from the straw mattress of Pete Maxwell's bed, and then the hiss of Garrett's breathing in the bedroom, anticipating the moment when Billy is finally killed by Garrett hiding in Maxwell's bed. Wrong gun: Garrett's is neither hanging from the wall nor coiled; and wrong bed, though still a bed in the West.

In all cases, the photographs present a picture of life that *appears* quieter, less violent than the stories they in fact document or the possible episodes from Billy's "life" that we seek to associate with them. The same is true of the remaining photograph, on page 13 of *the Collected Works*, borrowed from chapter 4 of *The Frontier Years*, "Soldiers – Red and White" (Brown and Felton 1955: 111, photograph 53). Its title is "Grave of Colonel Keogh"; the reproduction in *The Collected Works of Billy the Kid* shows only a detail of it, but the story that the photo tells is revealing. It documents the gruesome duty that befell a group of troopers who were sent in 1877 to the area where the battle of Little Big Horn had been fought in 1876. Rain and animals had uncovered many of the badly interred bodies of Custer's soldiers, and the group's task was to re-inter the bones properly. The troops chosen for this duty also included the few survivors of the battle. Identifying the bodies of the 7 officers that were to be removed for reburial elsewhere was difficult; some of the graves had been marked the previous year, but when they came to Custer's body, the first bones they picked turned out to be those of a corporal; the second body they found seemed to be the right one, and was placed in the coffin ("Caddle states in later years that they found another body and placed it in a coffin – 'I think we got the right body the second time'"). Apparently all that was left was "one thighbone and the skull attached to a part of the skeleton trunk" (Brown and Felton 1955: 112).

Bodies were found and re-buried, but they may have been the wrong ones; episodes of mistaken identity in death and in dying ("I believe you have killed the wrong man," says deputy sheriff Poe in his account of Billy's capture, qtd. by Ondaatje on page 103) echo through the legend of Billy the Kid, reputed dead while he was still alive, washed away by water in death, probably confused with other bodies, buried and reburied so that no one quite knows where his remains are (Tatum 1982: 12). All that is left of him, "if you dug him up and brought him out" would be: "the buck teeth," "a trail of vertebrae like a row of pearl buttons off a rich coat down to the pelvis," "arms [...] cramped on the edge of what was the box," "fine ankle bones," a bullet that would "roll in the skull like a marble," "the silver from the toe of each boot" – and the legend of the hundred of stories like a "jungle" in which he sleeps (Ondaatje 1970b: 97). But of course there is always the risk that "the box" may contain the wrong body – Michael the Kid instead of Billy the Kid entering the empty frame, for example.

In fact, Huffman's photograph of the soldiers is not even Huffman's: "The photographs of this battlefield are from negatives acquired by Huffman during his first years in Montana." They appear to have been taken by the photographer Stanley J. Morrow, though the negatives have since formed part of Huffman's collection (Brown and Felton 1955: 112, 244, No. 28).

In the original photograph, the officer who, in Ondaatje's reproducetion, appears to be about to walk out of the frame on the left is in fact staring at the grave of Colonel Keogh, marked by a wooden cross on which we make out the following words: "Col Keogh/and 28 soldiers/of/Co I 7 Cav/killed/here/June 25/1876." The wooden marker of the grave with its inscription must be left out of the reproduction in *The Collected Works* because it would otherwise show that the photograph refers to an episode that, while it is still about a war and the frontier, has nothing to do with Billy the Kid or the Lincoln County war. Yet the photograph and the "Credits" that allow us to trace it are there, partially and obliquely signalling the interconnectedness of different forms of living and dying on the frontier, of the myth of the frontier itself. The selection of this photograph brings into the book, albeit indirectly, the violence of other wars that have shaped the American consciousness, the death of soldiers, the plight of native Indians, those that have often been written out of the story and of history. "Col Keogh/and 28 soldiers" are now written out of this story by the cropping of the photograph. The story behind it also tells us that the remains of the officers were sought and re-buried under their names, whereas the many nameless soldiers did not receive the same privilege: Brown and Felton's note to the photograph reads: "*Captain Keogh's* bones were removed from the battlefield (along with those of several other officers) and were buried at Auburn, N. Y., on October 25, 1877. The officer in the foreground was Lieutenant Henry. J. Nowlan" (255).[9] Only the officers receive attention and a name; the rest are forgotten. There may be a more direct link than it might at first appear between this early postmodern book and Ondaatje's later, more explicitly engaged, *Anil's Ghost* with its exploration of violence, oppression and human rights through the digging up and identification of the remains of an unknown man.

9 Note to photograph 53.

Susan Sontag's description of photography as *memento mori* can be applied to this image almost literally (1979: 16). In the foreground of the photograph as printed in *The Collected Works*, bottom centre at the feet of the officer, we notice a skeleton. The position of these bones transforms the photograph into a picture of *vanitas* and a kind of anamorphosis that may call to mind one of its most famous examples, Holbein's *The Ambassadors*. Through the manipulation of the photograph, cropping it so that the bones are at the bottom centre (and thus making the image a universal symbol of mortality rather than the document of an individual death – the Colonel's – or of a specific historical episode – the extermination of Custer's soldiers), Ondaatje transforms the photograph into a *picture*, a representation of iconic rather than indexical type. Although not technically an anamorphosis, the effect is similar. The low contrast and definition require us to study the picture some instants longer before spotting the *vanitas* at its centre. The officer (a state representative, like the ambassadors) rather than the common soldier is foregrounded, a reminder of the vanity of the world, of the battle, of the wars, of the very rituals we perform in front of the spectre of death. *The Collected Works of Billy the Kid* itself, indeed, starts with a picture of *vanitas* and, as a book, can be treated as a giant anamorphosis that requires us to look at it askew to "see" what it may represent.

None of Huffman's photos have the flatness, the lack of contrast and detail of the reproductions in *The Collected Works of Billy the Kid* (especially in later editions than the House of Anansi's): they are not just "sharp in the main" as Huffman claims of his photographs of passing horses: they are, simply, "sharp." But none of the photographs chosen by Ondaatje for his book was taken from a horse in motion despite what the words on page 5 seem to suggest, and none of their subjects were moving when photographed. Ondaatje displays an almost perverse care in his choice of pictures of unmoving subject; it is their cropping that makes it look as if their subjects were moving: a wolfer that appears to be travelling on a cart with his dog, but the cart is stationary; an officer who looks like he is walking out of the frame, but is standing still. We know that for Huffman "men walking are no trick" (Ondaatje 1970b: 5), but in *The Collected Works* men walking are indeed a trick. For Huffman the residual fuzziness round the edges was a problem to overcome; for Ondaatje it becomes a bonus, even a trait to be enhanced in all photos. It conveys a greater sense of authenticity: we expect old photographs not to be too clear. As Sontag points out, old photographs increase our belief in their authenticity, they augment the aesthetic and affective value we attribute to them; indeed, the greater the fading or fraying, the more we value them (1979: 21, 141). The fuzziness of course also allows Ondaatje both to evoke the difficulty of fixing Billy into a single clear image and to link the photographs to Huffman's success in his experiments with moving subjects – that is to say, to the history of photography and film and the history of the search for an ever more exact representation of reality. Yet the images themselves, and the technology of the time, allowed for greater clarity than these images let on: if we accept that the quality of the reproductions is intentionally lower than that of the originals, then we also have to accept that we are the object of a joke, of an illusionism greater still than the illusionism of photography; an illusionism that is similar – though these are real photos of real nineteenth-century subjects – to the illusion that we are looking at nineteenth-century pioneers when we are in fact staring at Ondaatje's friends Sally and Stuart Mackinnon. Early photographs, in any case, were often retouched, composed from multiple negatives, fulfilling an aesthetic aim as much as an ethical drive towards truth-telling.[10] Ondaatje's structuring of the photograph on page 13 so that it becomes a representation of *vanitas* is, in a way, more faithful to the principles of early photography than we may at first think.

Another photograph and another photographer need to be acknowledged, although they have not appeared in more recent editions than the first and are not mentioned in the "Credits": Eadweard Muybridge is undoubtedly the most famous pioneer of photography of moving subjects, in particular men and horses, and the cover of the first edition reproduced one of his images – the positive on the front cover, and the negative (or its mirror image) on the back. (It is an interesting appendix to my previous discussion of the cropping out of subjects from history and their recovery to it that none of the histories of photography cited in the last footnote mentions Huffman, while they all discuss Muybridge's work, whereas Ondaatje chooses to credit the former, but not the latter). The use of this image in *The Collected Works of Billy the Kid*, taken from the sequence "'Pandora' jumping a hurdle, saddled, rider nude" (Muybridge 1979: Vol. III, pl. 644, 1308-9), evokes the process through which photography evolved into film, while the back cover evokes the photographic process whereby any image is revealed from its negative, its opposite: light-writing that needs to be developed in darkness so that the image can come to light again. Thus the cover images anticipate many of the book's themes: the oppositions of

[10] Cf. e.g. Mike Weaver, "Artistic Aspirations and the Lure of Fine Art," in Frizot (ed.), 185-95; Peter Turner, *History of Photography* (Twickenham: Hamlyn, 1987), esp. chap. 3, "Beauty and Truth: Pictorialism, Realism and the Fight for Photography as a Fine Art," 57-76; Naomi Rosenblum, *A World History of Photography* (New York, London and Paris: Abbeville Press, 1984), esp. chap. 5, "Photography and Art: The First Phase 1839-1890," 208-43.

stillness and movement, light and darkness, photography and film, the possibility itself of representation, the figure of the man and the horse that in the book, and in the Western genre, form almost a single being. John Cooke comments that both the front cover photograph and the back cover negative are "in two tones so that the horse and rider can be appreciated only in their roughest outlines. The suggestion of this cover, confirmed in the book, is that no sharp image of a moving subject – Billy the Kid – will emerge" (Cooke 1996: 191). Huffman's words on page 5, which we are invited to read as a caption for the empty frame above them, may in fact also refer back to the photograph on the cover. Of course they do not, originally: they are Huffman's words, not Muybridge's, and refer to the former's photographs, not the latter's (and to Bessie, not Billy); but their referent expands through the re-positioning of the citation; and, after all, when we encounter these words (if we are lucky enough to hold in our hands the Anansi edition), Muybridge's is the only photograph that we have seen so far. References and subjectivities merge, moving out of the book to its cover, making Huffman and Muybridge (the photographer that shoots from the horse and the one that took photographs of a horse) mirrors of each other, collaborators on the frontier of photography.

One of the surprises of early photography as soon as it acquired the technical ability to control the speed of the shutter was that it allowed man to perceive what the naked eye could not. Photography revealed aspects of reality that had so far remained invisible: whether a horse at a trot lifted all four hooves; the shape of a drop hitting a surface. To capture movement in real time, the camera had to move faster than the human eye, both in the way it fixed fragments of motion and in the way it then reassembled them into continuous movement (thus paving the way for motion pictures). Initially, people did not believe the "truthfulness" of photographs of animals or men in motion, as what they saw captured on the print was sharply different from what their eye was accustomed to perceiving; it was only when the images were then re-assembled in the magic lantern or zoopraxiscope and shown in sequence that the familiar could be perceived again, and belief returned.[11] Thus photography, like a historical anamorphosis, changed perception and made reality stranger, more mysterious, also provoking a crisis, or at last

[11] "In [Muybridge's] demonstrations, the audience was usually shocked by the revelation of the awkward movements that Muybridge's stop-motion photographs revealed, and then thrilled when, by means of the zoopraxiscope, they saw that the ungainly attitude of an instant did indeed form an integral part of what had always been regarded as graceful movement." Anita Ventura Mozley, "Introduction to the Dover Edition" (Muybridge 1979: Vol. 1, xxiv).

a debate, for realist painters.[12] The principles of realism demanded that painting should be as accurate a reproduction of what the eye saw as was technically possible; indeed, the development of techniques to achieve such exactness was one of the main pursuits of realism since the Renaissance, from the introduction of perspective and vanishing point to the use of camera obscura. However, photography showed not only that realist painting was not precise, but that the eye itself did not see accurately. Similarly, biography and autobiography are, traditionally, considered to be realist genres in which the match between reality and its representation has to be as close as possible, and in which the use of photographs, also based on a similar assumption, is often taken to underpin such match. In fact neither the eye in its perception of external reality nor the I in its perception of the self are accurate. By using photographs and the language of photography in his fictional (auto)biography of Billy the Kid, Ondaatje invites us to query the assumptions that underpin realism in the representation both of external reality and of the self. As Barthes says, there is no doubt that "*Ça-a-été*"; what remains in question is the nature of the *Ça*, and it is on this identification that our imaginary, our distortions, the myths that we construct and passively accept exercise their power. It is not fortuitous that Ondaatje's photographic sequence ends with him as a child, dressed as a cowboy, and a self-identification with the myth of the West. This query of realism however takes place within the framework of a commitment to the real, the historical and the documentary that much postmodernist criticism has traditionally viewed with scepticism. While many rightly point out the text's postmodernist fragmentariness, for instance, even here it is possible to link the book's structure with the context of early motion photography, and the way the many discrete, awkward-looking pictures taken by Muybridge and others of subjects in motion, once shown again in sequence in the magic lantern or zoopraxiscope, yielded a "realistic" picture that enabled the observer to recognise reality. *The Collected Works of Billy the Kid* achieves a similar synthesis of its fragments into a sense of narrative and aesthetic completeness, roundedness, where estrangement and alienation lead to the possibility of new perception and a new understanding of reality. It may be difficult, at first glance, to see what integrated vision may be granted by *The Collected Works*, but a retrospective critical synthesis

12 Cf. e.g. Mozley, xxiv; Turner, 16. In Rebecca Solnit's words: "Muybridge created a crisis of representation for realist painters: they had always insisted that they represented their subjects with maximum accuracy, but that accuracy had always been based on the observations of the eye. […] The eminent academic painter Jean-Louis Meissonier […] declared, 'All these years my eyes had deceived me' [and concluded in despair,] 'Never again shall I touch a brush!'" (Solnit 2003: 196-7).

that draws together the awkwardly disjointed images, texts, visions and hallucinations forces upon us a reflection on the way we have traditionally construed reality, the self, the myths by which we live, the boundaries that define the subject, the human, justice, law, violence, death. Susan Sontag has argued that photography constitutes a grammar and an ethics of seeing: I would suggest that the photographs and the language of photography in *The Collected Works of Billy the Kid*, together with its exploration of the subject, fulfils a similar function and also becomes an ethics of seeing (and I take "seeing" in both the perceptual sense and the cognitive, two meanings that become inseparable in the book). The framed white picture at the beginning of the book is both the absence and the presence of Billy; both the impossibility of capturing, fixing him, and the necessity of making a *tabula rasa* of our minds and of our preconceptions in order not just to re-imagine Billy, but to learn to "see" reality again, and what had previously been invisible to us.

CHAPTER 2

Light Writing, Light Reading: Photography and Intersemiotic Translation in Michael Ondaatje

Jeffrey ORR

Beykent University, Istanbul, Turkey

Much has already been said about the nature of photographic material in Michael Ondaatje's work, particularly in his early long poem, *The Collected Works of Billy the Kid.* I will focus here on an aspect of his work that has received less critical attention – that of photographic translation. While photographs are important to both *The Collected Works of Billy the Kid* and *Anil's Ghost*, they operate in different ways in those texts from the books this essay examines, namely, *Coming Through Slaughter, Running in the Family*, *In the Skin of a Lion*, and *The English Patient.* The *OED* defines "translate" as "to bear, convey, or remove from one person, place or condition to another," or "[t]o interpret, explain; to expound the significance of." In a more specific, literary context, Pamela Banting uses the term "intersemiotic translation" to describe a translation between two different types of media (1995: 11). All these definitions will be useful here. "The leap from one imagination to another can hardly be made" (1983: 81), writes Ondaatje in *Running in the Family*, but *hardly* is not *not*, and Ondaatje's work uses photographic translation as a means of accomplishing that leap, of moving between imaginations by moving between media. Susan Holbrook, in her description of "the erotics of translation" (1997: 232) in Nicole Brossard and Daphne Marlatt's work, asserts that "they have performed some of the most successful traversals of the problematic bridges between body and text, desire and language" (1997: 233). Such traversals are also made in Ondaatje's translational writing – in a different context, but dealing with similar issues of the body, text, language, and desire.

My argument here is that Ondaatje uses intersemiotic translation, approached through the body, to produce a situation in which the relationship between the characters and the narrator sets an example of how to approach the text and the past. The translations in Ondaatje's work demonstrate different ways of approaching artefactual evidence from the past, such as photographs. His work deals with "the unofficial story [...] a personal, complicated view of things" (Ondaatje qtd. in Bush 1994: 247), approaching characters from directions that have been cut off by attempts to "constitute the 'self' as a proprietary entity which can be conceived of as the rightful owner of an identity that is quantifiable, legislatible, and disciplinary," based on a notion of identity in which "the subject is stable, continuous, fully self-cognizant, and consequently capable of assuming a 'truth' value" (Dawson 2000: 50). Ondaatje's work undertakes intersemiotic translations as a way of finding meaning in the movement between the visual and verbal. The translation speaks back to the original, and invites the reader to consider particular elements in it from an altered perspective by producing "self portraits and possible fictional portraits" (Ondaatje qtd. in Bush 1994: 241) through a form that "reflect[s] as fully as possible how we think and imagine. And these keep changing, of course" (Ondaatje qtd. in Bush 1994: 243).

Translation often compares and contrasts the original to the translation, and there is a material sense in which the existence of the source text precedes that of the translation. In the sense of a source text, however, an "original" is dependent upon the translation for its existence, since it is not an original until some derivative is made from it. Here the translation is necessary for the production of the original just as surely as the original is necessary for the production of the translation. In terms of reading, too, the ways in which the texts mean is altered in both cases by the mutual relationship between the "original" and the "translation," since new ways of reading both texts arise from their differences and similarities. As Ian Fairley points out, "[e]very translated text may be activated as a newly translating text, "taken across" in order to gloss its original. The original may also gloss the translation" (2000: 1040). I take this as pointing to the ways in which the two texts invite comparison and re-evaluation of each other, so the translator's activity redefines both texts and allows the reader to be drawn into the position of translator as well, shuffling back and forth between the texts in a search for meaning and understanding. Translation is a mode of understanding, and of rewriting or rereading through one's own understanding.

Making Faces

The two clearest examples of photographic translation in Ondaatje's work are perhaps the best place to start. The honeymoon photograph of Ondaatje's parents from *Running in the Family* (1983: 163, fig. 1) is perhaps the best known example. In the preceding section "Photograph" (1983: 161), Ondaatje describes the image, noting that his parents:

> both begin to make hideous faces. My father's pupils droop to the south-west corner of his sockets. His jaw falls and resettles into a groan that is half idiot, half shock (all this emphasized by his dark suit and well-combed hair). My mother in white has twisted her lovely features and stuck out her jaw and upper lip so that her profile is in the posture of a monkey (161).

While the passage may be read as simple description, that description reveals the importance of particular elements of the image for the narrator: the contrast between Mervyn Ondaatje's facial expression and personal grooming, for example. The description continues, "[e]verything is there of course. Their good looks behind the tortured faces, their mutual humour, and the fact that both of them are hams of a superior sort [...] My father's tanned skin, my mother's milk paleness, and this theatre of their own making" (162).

Hutcheon points out the analogous relationship between the narrator's desire to find "the intimate and truthful in all this [...] to talk to all the lost history like that deserving lover" (1985: 54), and the reader's desire for an intimate relationship with the book. She argues that Ondaatje's narrative description of the image as "the photograph I have been waiting for all my life" (1983: 161) echoes a reading position in which "[w]e too have been waiting, if not all our lives, at least for 135 pages of fragments, for this look at the couple" (Hutcheon 1985: 305). However, she also claims the description that precedes the image makes the image "of course, [...] redundant: words can be as real as photographic reproducetions" (305). The situation is not quite so clear cut, however. The description of the honeymoon photograph, unlike the image itself, positions the narrator as a reader, describing his sense of belonging and intimacy, his reading of the image, and demonstrating a way of reading – "that great intimate act between reader and author, reader and book" (Ondaatje qtd. in Bush 1994: 240). It provides an example to the reader of how to approach the text that emphasises intimacy while challenging truth value.

The reading that Ondaatje provides before the appearance of the image is rich in description, and presented with obvious tenderness towards the subjects of the photograph. Its appearance before the image invites the reader to approach the image in the same way, with the tender affection of a family member, thereby inviting the reader to read through the body – to look at the image through the narrator's eyes, and approach the image from the perspective of a family member. In effect, it fulfils the narrator's stated desire from the opening pages by taking the people from the past "who stood in my memory like frozen opera" and "touch[ing] them into words" (1983: 22). This technique of looking through someone else's eyes is an important element in the way that Ondaatje's work approaches the understanding of the past. As Fairley asserts

> [i]n my experience translation is a way of coming to know the poem [...] The poem may be on the horizon of translation, but it's only in crossing that horizon that understanding can fully, physically, begin. For me, then, entering into the poem can't easily be told apart from its translational reinvention" (2004: 20).

By reinventing the image through translation, Ondaatje's work, too, encourages a physical understanding of it.

The intimate approach to the past in Ondaatje's work, however, is not the same as the official histories. It does not quantify or discipline the past, or assign it a stable subjectivity. Like the narrator's intimacy with the couple in the photograph, our intimacy with it as readers is provisional and indefinite. The description of his parents as ham actors in a theatre of their own creation (1983: 162) not only highlights the performative and fluid nature of identity, but serves as a warning to the reader that a definitive, disciplined "truth" may be out of reach. Instead of the forensic approach of the detective characters that constantly re-appear in his work, Ondaatje's work invites the reader to look for something more – the "well told lie [that] is worth a thousand facts" (1983: 206).

The picture from Ondaatje's parents' honeymoon both conceals the "truth" of the subjects' identity beneath the masks of their grimacing faces, and opens an ambiguous way of understanding their personalities. As ham actors who live life as theatre, the masks they wear both conceal their "true" identities, and are an important part of their identities. Ondaatje's narrator leaves the paradox unresolved, declining the imposition of a fixed, proprietary identity in favour of multiple, shifting possible identities. He describes his father as "one of those books we long to read whose pages remain uncut" (1983: 200), then notes that the book itself "again is incomplete" (201).

Loosening the Frame

The narrator provides a model of how to read in the passages above, and such a reading position demonstrated by the narrator also appears in another photographic translation from *Coming Through Slaughter.*

While the picture of the protagonist Buddy Bolden with his band is not included in the body of the text, its appearance on the title page of the book (fig. 2), and its repeated referencing in the story, gives some indication of its importance to the project of the work as a whole. It is the starting point for the entire narrative and imaginative project in which Ondaatje as narrator attempts to "push my arm forward and spill it through the front of your mirror" (1998: 135).

The translation of the image of Bolden and the band performs a similar function to the honeymoon picture in *Running in the Family.* It positions the narrator as reader, and produces a rhetorical stance in which the reader is called upon to approach the image in an analogous manner to that of the narrator – hence the direct address as the translation of the photograph is introduced:

> There is only one photograph that exists today of Bolden and the band. This is what you see.

Jimmy Johnson on bass	Bolden	Willy Cornish on valve trombone	Willy Warner on clarinet
	Brock Mumford on guitar		Frank Lewis on clarinet

(1998: 63)

Benjamin, in "The Task of the Translator," notes that the "essential quality" of a work of art "is not statement or the imparting of information. Yet any translation which intends to perform a transmitting function cannot transmit anything but information – hence, something inessential. This is the hallmark of bad translations" (1992a: 70). By Benjamin's standards, then, this is a good example of a bad translation. Ondaatje follows his photographic translation with the statement that, "As a photograph, it is not good or precise, partly because the print was found after the fire. The picture, waterlogged by climbing hoses, stayed in the possession of Willy Cornish for several years" (1998: 63). This description of the original photograph could equally well apply to the linguistic representation it follows. As a photograph, *it* is neither good nor precise. In the context of the novel, however, it's interesting for a number of reasons. Against the inessential information of a bad translation, Benjamin juxtaposes the idea that "[t]ranslatability is an essential quality of certain works, which is not to say that it is essential that they be translated; it means rather that a specific significance inherent in the original manifests itself in its translatability" (1992a: 71). The translation focuses attention on that "specific significance."

The situation with the image of Buddy Bolden and the band from *Coming Through Slaughter* is slightly different from that of *Running in the Family*, in that the presentation of the image precedes the literary translation. Here again, however, the differences between the two versions are significant, in that the visual and literary versions speak to each other, and the differences between them reveal new ways of reading the subjects. Like the translation of the honeymoon photograph from *Running in the Family*, the translation is a re-reading of the image, and an invitation to the reader to "come with me I want to *show* you something. You come too. Put your hand through this window" (1983: 89).

In the photograph Bolden is second from the right in the back row. Although he might not, initially, stand out from the rest of the band, the central vertical axis formed by the fold in the backdrop sheet and the angle formed by the neck of Johnson's bass and Cornish's trombone, with Bolden at its apex, do position him at the intersection of two major geometrical forms in the photograph, drawing the eye to his figure. The translation dispenses with the background and most of the nuances of the photographic blocking, focussing instead on the figures and their instruments.

The two neat lines of text in the translation, and their positioning on the page, read in a manner opposite to that of the photograph: the reader's eye first encounters not the subjects in the foreground of the photograph, but those in the back row. The words on the page acting both as signifiers and signifieds reverse the prominence of the figures, substituting strong horizontals for the insistent verticals of the photograph. Sobieszek argues that a strong vertical axis has been the historical norm in portraiture, and links it to conceptions of rationality, social hierarchical power, and unitary identity (1999: 254), noting that since the 18th century, "erectness equalled rectitude, a notion that still permeates our [i.e. Western] culture" (254). The horizontal, on the other hand, he links to an undermining or confounding of such ideals, implying that it connotes a more generous and egalitarian sense of interpersonal communication (256-80). In the honeymoon photograph from *Running in the Family* the vertical lines of Ondaatje's parents' faces are skewed in an act of subversive humour; the translation of the photograph in *Coming Through Slaughter* takes a similarly horizontal approach, which also subverts rationality, social hierarchical power, and unitary identity (1998: 254).

The most important change in the literary version is, perhaps, Bolden's coronet. In the photograph, the instrument is partially hidden behind Brock Mumford's head, and partially obscured by the fading of the print. In the translation, the instruments they play are the only defining characteristics of the subjects, and Bolden stands out by not being similarly identified with his instrument. By not including Bolden in this form of identification, Ondaatje not only further isolates him from the other band members, he also disassociates him from his music, and the instrument which eventually destroys him. Bolden, in the story, describes his return to New Orleans in bleak terms: "Then later Webb came and pulled me out of the other depth and there was nothing on me. I was glinting and sharp and cold from the lack of light. I had turned to metal at the mouth" (1998: 112). His return to the city is also his return to playing music, the combination which precipitates his slide into madness, and this passage describes him in terms of his instrument: glinting, sharp, and cold. He is undergoing a physical transformation ("metal at the mouth") into the instrument which corresponds to the alteration in both his public and private persona. He is being pushed into the identity of musician which he had previously shed, and becoming his horn; the other aspects of his life, including family, employment, and friends, falling away as his musical reputation spreads. The absence of the horn separates him from his historical identity as a musician, allowing other possible modes of identity to operate through the text.

Breaking Mirrors

Rather than producing a definitive portrait of the protagonist, *Coming Through Slaughter* refuses to pin Bolden's character to a stable subject position. Instead, the material translation of the image into the word points to another sort of translation, an imaginative movement from one body to another. Ondaatje's narrative voice frequently discusses the process of writing as an imaginative act that is intimately connected to the physical.

Beginning with narrator's realisation that when Bolden went mad, "he was the same age as I am now," a sense of physical interaction develops throughout *Coming Through Slaughter* as:

> [t]he photograph moves and becomes a mirror. When I read he stood in front of mirrors and attacked himself, there was a shock of memory. For I had done that. Stood, and with a razor-blade cut into cheeks and forehead, shaved hair, defiling people we did not wish to be. He comes in to the room, kneels in front of the mirror, and sits on his heels. Begins to talk. Holds a blade between his first two fingers and cuts high onto the cheek (1998: 135).

The identifying pronouns in this passage work to break down the distinction between Ondaatje and Bolden, moving from a "he" for Bolden and an "I" for Ondaatje to a "we" that joins them in an act of stripping away social identities and subjectivities, so that the "he" that follows in describing the act of self-mutilation is indeterminate, and can refer to either Ondaatje or Bolden, merging them in the act of cutting away identities.

Like the Bolden of the translation, then, the narrator strips away imposed personas, opening ambiguous possibilities for identity and identification, including identification with the characters in the book. The two strands intersect at several points, such as:

> Bolden's hand going up into the air
>
> in agony.
>
> His brain driving it up into the
>
> path of the circling fan.
>
> This last movement happens forever and ever in his memory (1998: 138).

The page layout with the small rectangular block of text and its accompanying caption reminds one of a photograph in an album. The album, however, gives no clue as to the context of the image or referent of the second pronoun "his," which can be read to refer to a memory of Bolden's, or a haunting image in the narrator's stuck in the narrator's head.

The closing passage of the book operates in a similar manner. Having described Bolden's existence in the state mental hospital through narrative, interviews, and archival inclusions, the book ends with the lines "I sit in this room. With the grey walls that darken into corner. And one window with teeth in it. Sit so still you can hear your hair rustle in your shirt. Look away from the window when clouds go by. Thirty one years old. There are no prizes" (1998: 160). Having noted earlier that Bolden went mad at thirty one, the same age as he is at the time of writing, Ondaatje ends with another ambiguously worded passage that can be read as describing either the narrator or the musician. In placing this indeterminate subject in that room with the single window, Ondaatje puts both himself and Bolden literally *in camera*, so that the book ends with the physical merging of the writer and the character, trapped in the setting of the photographic frame that opened the book. The merging of identities here, I'd argue, opens a means of understanding the historical personage of Bolden through shared bodily experience. Ondaatje describes his first encounter with Bolden through:

> [t]he thin sheaf of information. Why did my senses stop at you? There was that sentence, "Buddy Bolden who became a legend when he went berserk in a parade…" What was there in that, before I knew your nation your colour your age, that made me push my arm forward and spill it through the front of your mirror and clutch myself? Did not want to pose in your accent

> but think in your brain and body, and you like a weatherbird arcing round in the middle of your life to exact opposites (1998: 135).

The first point of interest in this passage is perhaps the use of the word "senses." The starting point for understanding the character here is the body, and the way in which the body reacts to the information, rather than the "cold facts" themselves, and the movement that enables the connection between the narrator and Bolden, like "[t]he leap from one imagination to another [that] can hardly be made" (*Running in the Family* 1983: 81), is a physical one, pushing and clutching in order to be able to "think in your brain and body" (1998: 135).

Seeing Through Another's "I"s

Similar processes are at work in *Running in the Family*, where Ondaatje calls himself into existence, putting himself as writer at the centre when concluding: "Half a page – and the morning is already ancient" (1983: 11). "The reader then learns [...] that the subject of Ondaatje's story is actually Ondaatje's father, that it is about his father land [...] Thus with his introductory gesture, Ondaatje makes himself the absent protagonist of his narrative" (Rothgerber 2005: 2). The same merging of identities occurs in that absence. Towards the end of the book, the narrator describes Mervyn Ondaatje "in front of his house now fully aware that the car was empty but for his body [...] a case of liquor under his arm" (1983: 188). The narrative then shifts pronouns, noting "[t]he absence of even an edge of the moon. Into the bedroom, the bottle top already unscrewed [...] The bottle top in my mouth as I sit on the bed like a lost ship on a white sea" (188). While this last line can be read as the voice of Mervyn Ondaatje speaking directly, there are none of the quotation marks or offset lines that indicate direct speech in the rest of the book. Moreover, the writing does not jump from one voice to another, but shades gradually from the one to the other: from the third person of the initial description, to the indeterminate movement "[i]nto the bedroom" with a noticeable absence of pronouns, and then into the first person. Here again, the narrator's identity gradually merges in to that of Mervyn Ondaatje, and the final "I" can be read as referring to either one.

The story of Ondaatje's father depends on an imaginative leap into his father's brain and body that is always provisional, and refuses closure. What makes it possible are not the known facts, although they certainly present a starting point. Rather, the bridge between consciousnesses across which this translational mode of understanding moves is intimacy. As the narrator puts it, "[n]ot that we ever thought we would be able to fully understand you. Love is often enough" (1983:

201). Ondaatje's work embraces multiple and indeterminate identities through an intimacy that relies on the body.

Benjamin, as noted earlier, points out that a bad translation transmits only information (1992a: 70). To understand someone fully in Ondaatje's statement here, means, I would argue, to replace the awareness of what Benjamin calls "specific significance" (71) with the collection of information, turning people into social commodities. Instead, as Brossard puts it, the book "seeks to understand the fragile ties that bind people together in intimacy" (1993: 179), noting that "to try to translate the magic that runs through *Running in the Family* [...] I travel towards what is most alive in myself" (179).

Group Work

This intimate approach to writing is an important aspect of the way that Ondaatje's work approaches the telling and gathering of stories. Ondaatje's work avoids the production of stable and disciplined representation by implementing a sense of communally produced identity that operates through the body. By considering people and the past as part of an ethical community, Ondaatje's work retains/asserts a respect for the fluidity of identity and the value of the individual beyond the ideological. The method is reflected in the way he considers the role of the writer. Where conceptions of the author, especially since the romantic era, have valorised the idea of the author as a lone creative genius who produces works individually, and with God-like control over the world of the book, Ondaatje implements a communal approach to writing in which the writer is less an author-god than a community scribe, as when "Women Like You" in *Running in the Family* is subtitled "the communal poem – Sigiri Graffiti, 5th century" (1983: 92). The difference is brought out in a number of his works. Ondaatje describes his early exposure to story-telling in a family setting as "a case of people one-upping each other at the dinner table [...] When I went back [...] I knew I wanted to talk to a lot of people, a lot of relatives [...] working on the book [*Running in the Family*] became a process of shifting that oral tradition into a literary form" (Ondaatje qtd. in Bush 1994: 239). The sense of the book as a group undertaking is reinforced in the "Acknowledgements" section at the end of the book with Ondaatje's opening assertion that "[a] literary work is a communal act" (1983: 205). It also appears in the beginning of the body of the work.

The opening section of *Running in the Family*, which, Nicole Brossard points out, "contains in miniature the book's most extravagant images" (1993: 181), describes the narrator's wish to touch his family into words as "[a] perverse and solitary desire" (1983: 22). It then goes on to consider the word "Asia" in distinctly embodied terms, both in the way the body produces the sound – "[t]he name was a gap from a dying mouth" (22) – and the aesthetics of the word as an embodied object which "sprawled" across the map, its vowels sleeping with the S (22).

These passages suggest a way of writing that works through the body and through intimacy. As Ondaatje asserts in the "Acknowledgements" section of the book, "a literary work is a communal act" (1983: 205). The "perverse and solitary desire" applies to a particular sort of authorial project and authorial control. Ondaatje's juxtaposition of these two ways of writing points away from authorial control, towards a conception of writing as engaged with others – other people and other times, other writers, other stories, other genres, other media.

That "perverse and solitary desire" of creativity is explored in Ondaatje's earlier *Coming Through Slaughter*, in the character of the photographer E. J. Bellocq. Bellocq's photographs of New Orleans prostitutes, and the description of their production, offer a counterpoint to the communal writing that Ondaatje embraces. Bellocq's approach to artistic creativity is the precise opposite of Bolden's. Bolden's music is produced with a band, hence communally. Bellocq's photographs, on the other hand, "were more on the level of fetish, a joyless, private game" (1998: 61). The problem with such a way of working is that "[t]he mystic privacy one can be so proud of has no alphabet or noise or meaning to the people outside" (61). If communication requires community, then this is precisely the element lacking in Bellocq's work.

If Bellocq can be taken as an example of the solitary writer, then he's not an example one would want to follow. Ondaatje points out that:

> [s]ome of [Bellocq's] pictures have knife slashes across the bodies. Along the ribs. Some of them neatly decapitate the head of the naked body with scratches. These exist alongside the genuine scars mentioned before, the appendix scar and others non-surgical. They reflect each other, the eye moves back and forth. The cuts add a three dimensional quality to each work (1998: 51).

Bellocq's defacement of the figures in the photographs blurs the division between photograph as the object and the image it presents, and, in a violent act of intersemiotic translation, echoes the scars on the bodies of the women portrayed in the scratches on the glass plates of the photograph and turns the two dimensional surface of the image into a three dimensional sculpture. "You can almost see the depth of the knife slashes" (51) writes Ondaatje, and the statement is sufficiently vague as to be able to refer to either the slashes in the plates or the "other, non-surgical" scars on the bodies of the women (fig. 3).

Bellocq's translations of his photographs into sculpture, like Ondaatje's, are certainly motivated by desire and bodily attraction, but do not have the interactivity or respect that characterises the act elsewhere in Ondaatje's work. Instead, they are acts of violence. He takes "[p]ictures. That were like... windows" (55, ellipsis original), framed to contain his subjects while he plays his violent private game with them, and separates the viewer from the viewed in both cases (window or daguerreotype) with a sheet of glass. Bellocq's work holds his subjects in the image: "snap. Lady with dog. Lady on sofa half naked. Snap. Naked lady" (51), and his fetishism is inhuman, mechanistic. The text describes Bellocq's face, the seat of his humanity (Sobieszek 174), as "[f]ace machinery. H Y D R O C E P H A L I C" (53). "You can think of Bellocq," Ondaatje writes, "wanting to enter the photographs, to leave his trace on the bodies. When this happened [...] he had to romance them later with a knife [...] the care he took defiling the beauty he had forced in them was as precise and clean as his good hands [...] The making and destroying coming from the same source, same lust, same surgery his brain was capable of" (51). This mechanistic, surgical lust is characterised by Bellocq's desire to leave *his* trace on the bodies, presumably while remaining untouched by them – as Ondaatje caustically notes, "he was too much of a gentleman" (51) to do so.

The fact that the bodily scars on the prostitutes and the sculptural scars on the photographic plates "reflect each other, the eye moves back and forth" (51) seems to indicate a breaking of the gaze, but it comes from our divided attention which shifts between the subject of the image and Bellocq as viewer, as if we are watching Bellocq looking at the image; rather than coming from an image that defies the gaze, our attention is divided between the two elements of the gaze, the viewer and the viewed. As readers, then, we are not so much involved in the production of the text ourselves as we are voyeuristically observing the power relationships that produce it. As readers, we are thus drawn into the same detached viewing position as Bellocq. Whereas, the final image of *Running in the Family*, can be read as an opportunity to see the world through Mervyn Ondaatje's eyes that opens up possibilities of engagement and intimacy, here we are placed in the position of viewing the world from the isolation that refuses any intimate connection to the world on which it gazes.

Widening the Scope

Translation also plays a role in Ondaatje's later works, in which visual images are not presented to the reader. Duffy relates the structure and content of *In the Skin of a Lion* to a number of historical documents and photographs in the City of Toronto archives. The project he undertakes can be read as a widening of Ondaatje's translational project. He points to a photograph of a cyclist and pedestrians crossing the newly-built Bloor Street Viaduct (fig. 4), the construction of which is a major element of the beginning of the novel, noting that the image "made it into the civic archives, [and] later (reduced to words) into *In the Skin of a Lion*" (1988: 128). Duffy's sense of reduction in intersemiotic translation reverses Hutcheon's comment on the honeymoon photograph from *Running in the Family*. There, the image is reduced to redundancy by the literary translation; here, the literary translation seems to offer an impoverished version of the image.

Duffy notes that "this item made it – sort of – into Ondaatje's novel" (127) in "one newspaper [that] had a picture of a cyclist racing across" (*In the Skin of a Lion* 1988: 143), which the protagonist, Patrick, encounters. Arguably, it could also be related to the earlier scene at the official opening of the bridge in which "a figure escaped by bicycle through the police barriers. The first member of the public. Not the expected show car containing officials, but this one anonymous and cycling like hell to the east end of the city" (1988: 27).

Duffy also unearths another archival photograph that bears a similarity to one described in the book (fig. 5) where "moisture in the tunnels appears white. There is a foreman's shirt, there is white lye daubed on the rock to be dynamited. All else is labour and darkness" (1988: 111). He is right to note that these images suit "one of Ondaatje's declared aims, that of returning to history the actualities of the workers experience, too often disregarded in quantitative assessments of a project" (126), and the narrator gives an example of how to carrying out that aim taken from photography.

There are, clearly, a number of photographic intertextual links in the book, but one of the most glaring is the reference to Lewis Hine. Hine's photographic valorisation of labour and empathetic depictions of child labourers, says a narrative voice addressing the reader directly, "betray official history and put together another family [...] his photographs are rooms one can step into" (145). *In the Skin of a Lion* could be described in similar terms, and does a similar job to the one he ascribes to Hine's photographs.

If *In the Skin of a Lion* takes archival photographs as one of its starting points, then, in altering them in the literary work, it also changes the way we read them, so that the "mental landscape and the personal story [...] wrestle against the documentary" (Ondaatje qtd. in Bush 1994: 243). The people described in the photographs dealt with here are still anonymous in the text, but that anonymity is of a particular sort. Their anonymity does not diminish their individuality, but rather invites the reader to reclaim them from the past, to join in the act of betraying the official history that has effaced them, and include them in the making of another family through the sort of imaginative leap described earlier. Again, there is a hint of how to go about this in the structure of the narrative. Patrick's discovery of the image of the cyclist in the newspaper is juxtaposed to earlier, official stories of the bridge's construction: "the shells of wood structures into which concrete was poured, and then the wood removed like hardened bandages to reveal the piers [...] survey arguments, the scandals, the deaths of workers fleetingly mentioned" (1988: 143-4). The passage opens with Patrick using a photograph of his partner, Alice, in an attempt to identify her in the newspaper, and ends with him turning the newspaper page to a photograph of bridge workers. "Third from the left, the newspaper said, was Nicholas Temelcoff" (144), a major character in the book's opening section. The passage thus bookends the anonymity of workers fleetingly mentioned or entirely effaced with characters who share that official anonymity but have been rescued from it by the narrative. The passage invites the reader to engage with the other characters in a similar manner, and to rescue them through a similar imaginative act. "Patrick," we are told, "never believed that characters lived only on the page. They altered when the author's eye was somewhere else [...] Each character had his own time zone, his own lamp, otherwise they were just men from nowhere" (143). Benjamin argues in "Theses on the Philosophy of History" that "[e]very image of the past that is not recognised by the present as one of its own concerns threatens to disappear irretrievably" (1992b: 247). The context of the presentation of these photographs "reduced to words" (Duffy 1994: 128), nonetheless invites the reader to expand them imaginatively, by making them a part of his or her concerns to rescue them from oblivion.

The Resistance of Memory

This approach to archival material, which betrays official history, is an important element in a translational reading of Ondaatje's later works such as *The English Patient*. The memories of *The English Patient*'s title character, Novak points out, perform "an act of translation by bringing forth into the language of the present the absences of the past" (1996: 207), but in an unstable and protean manner. Just as *Coming Through Slaughter* and *Running in the Family* have historical protagonists who remain beyond the scope of definitive knowledge, the Patient's past is ultimately indeterminate, produced through snapshot-like fragments of time and place. As Dawson asserts, "[a]lthough the detailed and intimate nature of the Patient's narrative suggests that he is likely to be Hungarian-born Count Ladislaus de Almásy, the title of the text and the narrator's use of both names preserve a degree of ambiguity" (2000: 72).

Ambiguous moments in which the past erupts into the present also structure the book on a smaller scale. The fragmentary nature of both *Running in the Family* and *Coming Through Slaughter* give the books the feel of a box of snapshots, in which an attempt at linear narrative will be disrupted by decontextualized moments and episodes that never quite fit together neatly. The "Honeymoon" section of *Running in the Family,* instead of the expected moment of romance, provides a list of contextual information from around the world including headlines about current events, the price of a bottle of beer, and the weather (1983: 37). The book also has sections which open with quoted dialogue, but no indication as to who is speaking (48, 53), and the section "Dialogues" (173-8) is composed entirely of direct reported speech without any indication of who is speaking. Likewise, *Coming Through Slaughter* includes recurrent images such as "[p]assing wet chicory that lies in the field like the sky" (1998: 57) that reappear in different contexts, and often with none at all.

The English Patient is full of similar fragmentary moments of time that intrude on the time of the narration, or capture representative instances and people with a sometimes photographic (though often filmic) consciousness. From the Patient's room the narrative jumps to "[t]he long Cairo evenings. The sea of night sky, hawks in rows until they are released at dusk arcing towards the last colour of the desert. A unison performance" (1996: 161). The Patient re-collects these fragments as he tries to piece his past together. "In 1930 we had begun mapping […] We were the desert Europeans," the Patient tells Hana, and then provides a set of literary snapshots as if handing her the pictures.

> John Bell had sighted the Gilf Kebir in 1917. Then Bagnold, who found his way to the south into the Sand Sea. Madox, Walpole of Desert Surveys, His Excellency Wasfi Bey, Casparius the Photographer […] And the Gilf Kebir – that large plateau resting in the Libyan desert, the size of Switzerland, as Madox liked to say (135).

Likewise, he jumps from philosophising about the desert's teachings to "1933 or 1934. I forget the year. Madox, Casparius, Bermann, myself, two Sudanese drivers and a cook" (139). These are collected fragments of a hazy past that have somehow gotten out of order.

Later, the drugged Patient recalls that

> When I went back to the desert, I took with me the evenings of dancing to the 78 of 'Souvenirs' in the bars, the women pacing like greyhounds, leaning against you while you muttered into their shoulders […] 1938.

> 1939. There was the whispering of love in a booth. There was war around the corner (243).

Labelled by year like a box of old loose photographs, the Patient's memories operate for both his listener, Caravaggio, and the reader, as markers of events that resist a closure of interpretation. Ondaatje's books, in the presentation of these small fragments that sit with minimal movement or context, encourage the reader to visualise the images, translating the literary into the visual.

By disrupting any attempt at linearity in the narrative, the fragments of the past disrupt the division between past and present, as well as any attempt to produce a linear historical narrative. In doing so, they also disrupt the construction of the Patient as a subject contained in a linear narrative, subverting the official identity that Caravaggio attempts to assign him. In the middle of the Patient's drugged recollections, the present of the story breaks in: "*Who is he speaking as now?* Caravaggio thinks" (244). Caravaggio's question, directed as much to the reader as to the character, is left unanswered, and the reader is invited to grapple with its implications for how much one can know about either history or identity.

Cook notes that the Patient "gradually frees himself from his specific time-bound identity and comes to identify instead with [...] the self that incorporates in one simultaneous space all the cumulative experiences of lost time" (1999: 48). This desire to free one's self from time and space while incorporating experience is precisely the photographic mindset that Sontag describes: "Photographs really are experience captured, and the camera is the ideal arm of consciousness in its acquisitive mood" (1977: 4-5). As Novak notes, such a position is "allied with the conventional construction of the Western male subject, the same one whose privilege is founded upon the patrilineal names and national identities the [Patient] claims to detest [...] Embedded within the Patient's narrative is a colonial world view that sees the non-Western world as empty and unexplored" (2004: 215-6). By structuring the Patient's narrative around these fragmentary and displaced moments from the past, the mode of telling of the Patient's memories undermines the very identity he exhibits in the anecdotes.

Caravaggio later describes the Patient as "this man, who speaks sometimes in the first person, sometimes in the third person" (1996: 247). The Patient's pronoun use thus becomes as important an issue as the narrators' indeterminate use of them in *Running in the Family* and *Coming Through Slaughter*. As in those books, the characters' identities merge in moments of shared understanding through shared experience. "All day they have shared the ampoules of morphine," we are told, and then, "each swallow of morphine by the body opens a further door, or he leaps back to the cave paintings or to a buried plane or lingers once more with the woman beside him under a fan, her cheek against his stomach" (247). As both characters are morphine users, the pronouns here can be read as describing either the Patient's memories, or Caravaggio's engagement with them, and the two characters' identities are conflated in the passage. The approach the text points to as a way of wrestling with the question is also similar to that suggested in other of Ondaatje's work. As the Patient tells Caravaggio, "When we came upon messages on our travels [...] he [Madox] would read it and then press his hand upon it as if to touch its possible deeper meanings, to become as intimate as he could with the words" (243). The body is the conduit through which the past becomes relevant to the present.

Photographic translation, in Ondaatje's work, is both a material process that moves an image into words, and a way of reading that allows understanding to begin with the body. It produces an exchange between texts that casts light not just on information, but on the "specific significance" that is brought out through the exchange between versions. In rereading and reinventing the translated text, it opens new possibilities for understanding texts and people in which, to return to Benjamin, "everything that has a history of its own, and is not merely the setting for history, is credited with life" ("The Task of the Translator" 1992a: 72). If the discourse that Ondaatje calls "official history" turns people into objects and actions into linear narrative, Ondaatje's work recognises that there is always more to a person than a subject position, more to an action than an explanation. It permits a partial understanding of identity that evades the final imposition of meaning and closure.

By merging identities, the bodies of the characters and the narrators perform a "leap between imaginations" (Ondaatje 1983: 81) that refuses distanced objectivity in favour of involvement and intimacy. Ondaatje's work also has a prescriptive element, however. The narrative approach serves as an example for us as readers; in Ondaatje's books, we are invited, through direct address and illustration, to carry on the act of translation and form our own connections with the past with the techniques of rereading and reinvention used in the novels. Ondaatje's work is thus not a form of passive entertainment, but an invitation to join the people in his books in, as Brossard puts it, "constantly escaping testimony, realism, the chronology of events" (1993: 181), and to work "on the side of beauty, of sensuality" (180) in producing a different way of understanding the past that brings it into the sphere of our own concern.

CHAPTER 3

Ladies and Gentlemen… Mr. Leonard Cohen: The Performance of Self, Forty Years On

Keith HARRISON

Vancouver Island University, Canada

Ladies and Gentlemen, Mr. Leonard Cohen, the National Film Board of Canada documentary that was instrumental in turning Leonard Cohen into an icon, began as another film. Its working title was "Four Poets," and the original notion was to follow Earle Birney, Phyllis Gotlieb, Irving Layton, and Leonard Cohen on their reading tour across Canada. However, the filmed result was reportedly so boring that this initial idea was scrapped (David De Volpi, "Telephone interview" 22 July 2005). Only as a revised project, "a re-edited and partially re-shot film by Donald Brittain" (Nadel 129), with a singular focus on the charismatic personality of Leonard Cohen, did the documentary gain enough dramatic energy to be produced.

Synchronised to the voice of the male announcer off-camera, "Ladies and Gentlemen…," the first part of the title appears in black on the white screen, and to continuing audio there is a visual projection of the concluding words of the emcee's introduction on a second line, "Mr. Leonard Cohen," as a young man wearing a black leather jacket, a white collar that has almost a clerical prominence, and a sweater leaving visible the top of a tie walks on stage. Shot respectfully from an upward angle, the poet as performer enters in response to the show-biz voice, whose words have a double function here of introducing both the on-stage personage and the filmmaker's subject – *and*, in retrospect, proclaiming the incipient fame of Cohen as a singer-songwriter since it is this very film that John Hammond viewed before deciding to meet and sign him for Columbia Records (Nadel 151).

Yet the young on-screen Cohen about to enter into much wider media consciousness gives off a kind of diffidence, a pre-celebrity tentativeness, even shyness, as his right hand with its closed fingers lifts to his mouth as if to cover a cough, while his left hand pins some loose papers to the top of a couple of books. He gives a quick look out at the camera and the audience, with both hands holding onto his reading material. Raising now the left hand to his lips, knuckles wiping furtively at his nose, Leonard Cohen inadvertently images winter – more than half a dozen years before Margaret Atwood's *Survival* – as a defining motif of Canada's cultural identity.

With the sound of clapping making an audio transition, the camera pans to the applauding people filling the seats of a modest, indoor amphitheatre. The film editor, Barrie Howells, then cuts to a low, near frontal shot of Leonard Cohen, who gives a barely perceptible nod and begins speaking without notes in an unhurried, muted voice that is almost one of adolescent withdrawal or – in its lack of clamorous self-hype – stereotypically Canadian.

In 1965, the year *Ladies and Gentlemen, Mr. Leonard Cohen* was released, Canada, too, had the semiotic contradictions of a perfectly knotted tie and a black leather coat. Two years later, this conflicted national self-image was forgotten as Canadians celebrated the summer of the nation's centennial like adolescents. Endless parties and ceaseless personal self-discoveries were features of a year that became instant mythology. At a time when the world was seeking peace and love and the United States was napalming Vietnam, Canada had as its Prime Minister, Lester B. Pearson, who had received the Nobel Peace Prize for resolving a crisis in the Middle East by the concept of a UN peace-keeping force. In 1968 he would be replaced by a figure even more charismatic than Cohen, and in that altered state of being labelled Trudeaumania, Canadians were finally freed from the metaphoric winter that had been an unreflective extension of geography. To our delight and surprise, we could see ourselves in the flattering mirror of Pierre Elliot Trudeau as bilingual, playful, cosmopolitan, witty, hedonistic, brainy, full of *élan*, and able to laugh at the country's bleak, inherited code of endurance. Suddenly, we remembered that two of the most exciting pianists ever, Glenn Gould and Oscar Peterson, were our compatriots, and along with Leonard Cohen, singer-songwriters like Joni Mitchell, Neil Young, Gilles Vigneault, and Robert Charlebois were emerging as compelling international voices. And English-Canadian writers, such as Alice Munro, Mavis Gallant, Mordecai Richler, Margaret Atwood, Timothy Findley, and Michael Ondaatje, were becoming conspicuous in the planet's print culture. This exhilarating cultural flowering included Northrop Frye, a literary critic and theorist of genius, and Marshall McLuhan, our guru of the media, who might have been extrapolating from Canada's ethnic mosaic when he coined the term, "global village." Somehow, the colonial anxieties that had frozen Canadians forever had melted away. With a new, naive sureness of direction, we modestly believed we were the compass to the future – as had been ludicrously predicted at the turn of the century by Prime Minister, Sir Wilfrid Laurier (1896-1911), who had announced, "The 20th Century belongs to Canada."

That utopian fantasy ended, however, in 1970 with the terrorist FLQ crisis involving kidnapping and murder and the imposition of the War Measures Act by Trudeau, and the impending fragmentation of the country. But for a few heady years, "the true North, exactly here," had been the jingoistic answer of many unflag-waving Canadians to the question, "Where are you supposed to be now?"

To that question Cohen in the film responds:

> I said in the cafeteria.
>
> They nodded to each other. Where are you supposed to be now?
>
> In the cafeteria [Cohen's voice louder, more intense].
>
> Well, you see as their questions continued, my answers which had started innocent enough began to sound like I were [a grammatical stumble and a fast revision] was protesting too much. In fact, after being interrogated more – three or four more times – I was shouting, pushing them aside, causing them to run after me down the corridor. It was only when a guard identified me that was I able to go back to my friend [pause] who had eaten my jacket. [the absurdist punch-line delivered, Cohen keeps a straight face. But at the full release of the audience's laughter, he ducks his head, raises the books and papers in his right hand, whose index finger traces down the length of his nose before touching his lower lip to partly hide his sideways grin – one of gratification and rapport with his fans – and possibly slight embarrassment?].

Cohen's fine performance has succeeded through musical pauses, concise modulation of details, and Zen-like wit. If jokes are a model for story-telling, it becomes evident that many of his poems and songs combine this off-beat narrative form with lyricism. In the staged and filmed presentation of self that opens *Ladies and Gentlemen*, Leonard Cohen manages to create laughter in the context of mental hospital melancholy, and shift the Canadian self-image from wintry cold to hipster cool.

The documentary bio-pic then cuts away from the public performance to an exterior shot of an urban scene, with pedestrians walking towards the camera. As in what Bill Nichols calls the expository mode, with its "voice-of God tradition" (105) and its "impression of objectivity" (107), an encapsulating male v.o. speaks over an upbeat jazz track: "Out of the crowds of Montreal has come a singular talent with four books under his belt and a growing reputation.

He is not primarily a stand-up comic but a novelist, a poet, and a very confident young man." Leonard Cohen walks towards the lens, with his dark, longish, partless hair that does not quite echo the androgynous look of the Beatles. The camera records him as he moves leisurely through downtown Montreal in what looks like the same leather coat. The v.o. changes as we hear Cohen reading from a poem: "My favorite cooks prepare my meals,/… and all my work go well" (with the tonally rich title omitted, "I have not lingered in European monasteries").

On this note of self-satisfaction, the film cuts to a shot of open fields, which are passing outside a car window, then to a 2-shot of Cohen sitting in the back seat of a car bantering with Irving Layton, his fellow poet and sometime mentor.

In Cohen's first on-camera interview, there is mention of a dead grandfather who was a poet: "He was becoming senile, but in his senility there were great lapses of poetry." Throughout the film, Cohen's acute sense of inversion, reversal, and paradox shows his ease with the art of the comedian (especially with what's known in the biz as the Allen Woody). His insights, often couched as jokes, possess a similar quality of linguistic surprise, and engage the viewer by playing off expectations of what is coming next. Cohen's very skilled and tactical voicing of language creates a Bakhtinian dialogism with the directors, shifting an ostensible film biography into fragments of an autobiography, allowing him to tell much of his life his own way. But by framing a photograph of Cohen's grandfather within the lens of the movie camera, the directors complicate this game of perception versus self-perception. Through bringing into visibility the communication of intergenerational images of the self, *Ladies and Gentlemen, Mr. Leonard Cohen* inquires into how identities are composed, fixed, transferred, and recomposed. In this celluloid remembrance, the poet and the filmmakers may have overlapping yet divergent motives.

The mirroring of grandfather and grandson, which is at once cinematic and existential, undercuts the Romantic idea of self-fashioning that Cohen usually projects. In response to the presence of the camera, the grandson quotes his grandfather in a retrieval that is also a re-creation, and a performance of a mini-scene: "'Oh, you're the writer,' as if he [the grandfather] had found some guarantee of the extension of his own soul." There is a poignant sense of distance between the dead, unknown grandfather in the static, elegiac photograph and the grandson whose words we listen to and whose on-screen movements we watch as participants in a shared act of celebrity-making, conferring on Leonard Cohen through our attentiveness a quasi-immortality. By quoting his ancestor out loud, he plays a double role in the re-enactment of family history, nudging the documentary towards a performance piece.

Although "documentary film" denotes objectivity, John Grierson – who coined this term "in a review in 1926" – also worked "as the first film commissioner in Canada" shortly after the outbreak of war in 1939 (Handling 775) and used the NFB for national promotion and propaganda. Similar contradictions may be discerned with respect to *Ladies and Gentlemen, Mr. Leonard Cohen* insofar as this flattering, sympathetic, and "truthful" portrait will be crucial in launching his recording career. Cohen as a filmed poet who performs himself is no naïve Nanook of the North biting down on a record to see how the sound of a voice got inside (Cf. Rothman 30-4). He's sophisticated enough to know that the documentary mode can double as a form of self-advertisement.

"What Types of Documentary Are There?" Nichols asks in Chapter 6 of his recent book, *Introduction to Documentary*.

The first kind that he discusses, the poetic, would seem appropriate for a cinematic study of a poet, but Nichols asserts that in this type directors typically treat people "on a par with other objects as raw material," and the emphasis is on the overall lyrical impressions of the filmmakers; "[s]ocial actors seldom take on the full-blooded form of characters with psychological complexity" (102). Such an approach obviously does not describe Donald Brittain and Don Owen's portraiture of Leonard Cohen, and yet the film itself, *Ladies and Gentlemen, Mr. Leonard Cohen*, could be categorised as a modernist work, and therefore has affinities to poetic documentary insofar it is "a way of representing reality in terms of a series of fragments, subjective impressions, incoherent acts, and loose associations" (103).

The second type analyzed by Nichols is the expository, with its authoritative v.o., which obtrudes several times in this film, including a summing-up near the end. "Expository documentaries rely heavily on an informing logic carried by the spoken word. In a reversal of the traditional emphasis in film, images serve a supporting role" (107). But a significant modification of this type should be noted: the voice-over heard most frequently in this documentary is Cohen's, not that of an omniscient narrator. The resulting ambiguity (if not ambivalence) concerning point-of-view means that the subject's internal voice doubles as external commentary, so the effect is often one of self-exposition.

The third type, the observational, associated with the work of Frederick Wiseman, "gives the impression that the filmmaker is not intruding on the behaviour of others" (111). Although there are moments in *Ladies and Gentlemen, Mr. Leonard Cohen* when the cameraperson appears "to be invisible and non-participatory" (112), more typically the viewer is conscious of the filming process through off-camera commentary, images of recording equipment, and obvious montage.

The fourth type, identifiable by the presence of interviews, is the participatory mode, which Nichol links to the Russian term, *kinopravda*:

> As "film truth," the idea emphasizes that this is the truth of an encounter rather than the absolute or untampered truth. We see how the filmmaker and subject negotiate a relationship, how they act toward one another, what forms of power and control come into play, and what levels of revelation or rapport stem from this specific encounter (118).

Key moments of the NFB documentary, such as those in the screening room scene near the conclusion, involve such direct, on-camera exchanges. Important also in this context is Cohen's written disclaimer on the bathroom wall, indicating a discrepancy between his actual life and real life.

From this sense of ontological gap, the reflexive type logically follows, where the filmmakers seek to make overt their construction of the film. As Nichols observes, "Instead of *seeing through* documentaries to the world beyond them, reflexive documentaries ask us to *see documentary* for what it is: a construct or representation" (125). The on-screen discussions of editing choices and the showing of out-takes make the conclusion of this film highly reflexive. By belatedly drawing attention to their own careful assemblage of words and images, the directors and editor amusingly problematise the preceding sense of realism – and trust – into which the viewers have been lulled.

Nichol's sixth and final type has been alluded to already: "Performative documentary underscores the complexity of our knowledge of the world by emphasizing its subjective and affective dimensions" (131). Consequently, this kind of film, like much of *Ladies and Gentlemen, Mr. Leonard Cohen* – from the showbiz intro onward – engages us through performance. In some cases, such as Cohen's pretending to be asleep, "[a]ctual occurrences become amplified by imagined ones" (Nichols 131). This kind of staging seems to contradict the premise of documentary, which is to record reality. However, as Caryl Flinn observes in her essay, "Containing Fire: Performance in *Paris Is Burning*":

> poststructuralist and postmodernist theory […] have cast the concept of preexisting 'reality' and its attendant notions of authenticity, truth, and objectivity into permanent question […]. In fact, it is no stretch to say that documentary films, in many ways more so than other cinematic forms,

> reveal the constructed – indeed, performative – nature of the world around us (429).

Cut to Leonard Cohen performing in front of well-dressed spectators in a tone-y room whose walls are covered with framed paintings: "His blood on my arm is as warm as a bird/ […] /Oh send out the raven ahead of the dove" (from "Prayer for Messiah," *Let Us Compare Mythologies* 18).

Cohen's black leather coat is beginning to look like a poet's uniform, a kind of costume. As such, this coat may be a symptom of Cohen's actorly condition of alienation, as analyzed by Walter Benjamin in "The Work of Art in the Age of Mechanical Reproduction":

> The feeling of estrangement that overcomes the actor before the camera […] is basically of the same kind as the estrangement felt before one's own image in the mirror. But now the reflected image has become separable, transportable. And where is it transported? Before the public. Never for a moment does the screen actor cease to be conscious of this fact. […] The cult of the movie star, fostered by the money of the film industry, preserves not the unique aura of the person but the "spell of the personality," the phony spell of a commodity (230-1).

As in some wish fulfilment dream tinged with nightmare, we could be watching the transformation of Leonard Cohen's own name into a brand name to be consumed.

Cut to a visual of a small box jutting out from a hotel wall. The audio coming through this intercom is of a working-class, Québecoise voice, one that ironically counterpoints the richly modulated accents of the film's male narrator. She announces it's "*onze heures*," and time to "*se lever*." Cohen, who is shown lying in bed under a coverlet with only his head visible, says "*Merci*" and gets up, goes to the window in his white t-shirt and underpants – an audacious and *risqué* shot for Canada back in 1965 – then smoothly pulls up the blinds and pushes down the window. Until the post-production segment much later in the film, the spectator does not sense that this self-exposure has been calculated and rehearsed, and what has just been viewed is, at best, a second take. In what is a *mise en abyme* for the entire documentary portrait, this moment of filmed reality with the blinds will be revealed as performance or contrivance, a kind of pseudo-intimacy.

As Cohen gazes out at two small dormer roofs layered by snow, first-time viewers do not anticipate how their faith in the truth of images will be dispelled at the film's end (accompanied by Cohen's own wry self-mockery). The camera, in what is a delayed establishing shot, then shows a whole city covered in snow while Cohen talks off-camera about hotels as sanctuaries "of a temporary kind," which make them "therefore all the more delicious." In 1983 this preoccupation would be expressed through an extended music video Cohen co-wrote, *I Am a Hotel*, about which Irving Layton quipped, "No identity crisis for Leonard Cohen." This 24-minute video, filmed at the King Edward Hotel in Toronto, follows the imaginative conceit of several hotel rooms remembering the lives of their guests who are given ghostly yet vivid presences by several performers who inhabit the love lyrics of five songs by Leonard Cohen, who, himself, plays the on-screen role of a long-time resident.

In the 1965 NFB film, Cohen speaks of hotels as providing "a very comfortable and anonymous, subtly hostile environment" – even as he abandons that anonymity by asking the camera to come inside his room. Back-stage and complicit with his fame-making, we as a privileged audience observe Cohen applying a kind of make-up to his face, PhisoHex acne-cream. *Ladies and Gentlemen, Mr. Leonard Cohen*, by having the camera pan past the bottle of skin ointment creates the illusion of private access to its subject. We now know how "the rise in the US of numerous television-based, hybrid formats has blurred the hypothetical line between documentary and fictional representation" (Berry-Flint 40-1). But long before the phenomenon of celebrity reality TV was developed commercially, the directors of this film offered a (now retro) glimpse of celebrity in progress: Leonard Cohen performing Leonard Cohen.

In 1989 I was paid by the NFB to publicise this film by updating – replacing – earlier copy (by an unknown writer) that read in part:

> The portrait presented by the film is informal. Mr. Cohen is shown walking the streets of the city, eating in a popular night spot, sleeping in his three-dollar-a-night hotel room, and even taking a bath. Wherever he is, and no matter what he is doing, there is little doubt of his primary interest in poetry and the poetic impulse.

The usage of the word, "informal," and the polite address, "Mr. Cohen," mark the decorum of Canadian society in 1965. By the time I wrote about this film twenty-four years later, the knotted-tie prose had (within the promotional space and constraints of the back of a video jacket) taken on the rebellious syntax and rhythms of a black leather jacket:

> This jazzy 1965 black-and-white film portrait catches the imaginative energies, lyrical and comic, of a young Leonard Cohen, the quicksilver poet, novelist, and songwriter.
>
> Designed, written and co-directed by Donald Brittain, this witty film classic presents Leonard Cohen – arguably the first and last romantic writer in English Canada – as the voice of the questing, hedonistic, pre-feminist sixties. On the verge of a pop stardom that would blur the boundary between

song and poem, Cohen here reveals the sources for his jewelled imagery of violence, yearning, despair and sexuality.

At once candid and elusive, he also unfolds his created self-image as lover and prophet, "Canada's Messianic hippie" in Louis Dudek's description. For the camera Cohen acts as both hero and anti-hero, lucid creator and wry derider of his own romantic myth. By doing so, he demonstrates how he shapes an engaging poetics of rapport, one that emerges, paradoxically, from a lyrical and sardonic concern with self.

Cut to a shot of a television monitor, then to the set of a TV show being filmed live, with Pierre Berton as its host and Cohen as one of its guests. To very reluctant television producers, Cohen had apparently insisted that he would only go on if the NFB crew could also be present (de Volpi). In this scene of media filming media filming, discussion becomes acrimonious. Layton weighs in to defend Cohen after Berton claims to be totally lost by Cohen's reference to the state of grace that a poet seeks.

Cut to a different interior setting with much visible technology, which in its outdatedness for viewers forty-odd years later creates a sci-fi spoof atmosphere. Continuity with the previous scene is achieved when a male on-camera questioner asks Cohen how he made out with Pierre Berton. The reply, "He really wanted me to cut my con out," voices a notion that will be examined further (and punned on later) in the documentary. Cohen, appearing dwarfed and victimised, goes into a sound room that looks like an immense, airless squash court in order to record poems for the archives. As he is about to consign the present moment to some vague future, he is warned that any "dirty word" will be deleted. Cohen objects, "Yeah, well, there are no dirty words ever," and he begins to read the first poem from *The Spice-Box of Earth*, "A Kite Is A Victim."

At the end of this reading, Cohen's own spoken word, "Cut," is used as the film cuts to the interior of a Montreal bistro: images of cigarette smoke, cable-stitched sweaters, bottles of Molson beer, and graffito: "Marita, please find me. I am almost 30." The writing on the wall, later published as a poem (*Stranger Music* 116), conveys a lostness and yearning that here is transmitted as a joke, but which may anticipate Cohen's intermittent Buddhist retreats from a public persona and career into a place of spiritual and literal silence. In this bistro scene, Cohen as emerging pop idol speaks the voice-over, and is thus positioned as his own Virgil to his own Dante. Externalised guide to his inner, mixed emotions of the infernal and the paradisal, he warns "there's a very particular glow that a hostile crowd emits," and that "the crowd is interested in consuming you in it, but sometimes on the other hand it's composed of some sort of fixative that is sprayed on you as soon as you walk in and you become very very much yourself." The tensions of this dualism, situated in the relationship of self to others, define social performance as either the loss of an interior self or, paradoxically, its expressive fulfilment.

As a half-comic transition to the next scene, the anonymous v.o. says, "Cohen has been in films since 1937," and the visuals cut to old home movies taken of him as a boy by his father who "instilled in his son an early fascination with photography and the pleasure of being photographed" (Nadel 16). These moving images show Cohen riding a tricycle and standing in front of the family car slightly to the foreground of the uniformed chauffer. The amateur cameraman has long disappeared into early death (Nadel 5-6), but the presence of these images acts as another *mise en abyme* in this self-reflexive NFB documentary that, several decades later, possesses a feeling of nostalgic distance comparable to his father's dated shots of his son. These images of the childish Cohen re-present themselves in an even more haunting manner in *I'm Your Man* (2005), which blurs the categories of bio-pic and concert film, and which within its *mélange* of performance, introspection, collaboration, re-voicings, and retrospection situates this footage at an almost maximal remoteness from the aged Cohen who is on-camera elsewhere.

In *Ladies and Gentlemen*, his father's footage is given additional resonance through his son's reading of lines written in response to this home movie, with "filmed" taking on its ironic meaning of "blurred":

> Here is the movie filmed with the bodies of his family
> his father aims the camera at his uncles
> tall and serious
> boutonniers in their dark lapels
> who walk too close and enter into blurdom.
> Now the boy and his cousins fight small gentlemanly battles
> the girls curtsey
> all the children are invited to leap
> one at a time across the flagstone paths.
> A battalion of wives is squeezed abreast
> is decimated by the edge of the screen
> His mother is one of the first to go.
>
> (my transcription)

Like many photographs, these moving images reminding us – as in Plato's allegory of the cave – of missing originals. "Although we may not think about it when we are watching a movie, the presence of the [cinematic] image always implies the absence of the object" (Corrigan and White 179). Cohen's poetic narration extends that notion of missingness even to the present-tense act of recording: "blurdom," "squeezed," "decimated," and "the first to go."

From a home movie segment of a very young Leonard Cohen skiing down a slope on Mount Royal – and, at the end, falling – the NFB film effects a transition through shots of winter trees to his off-camera reading of a poem about this park. Its probing, haunted words ask, "Has she ever been called a dirty Jew?"

This startling reference to anti-Semitism ruptures the visually innocent scene of children at play. A montage of images follows, accompanied by selections from Cohen's poetry as voice-overs that encompass the range of his experience: Westmount, night shots of the city, the signing of books (that seemingly unavoidable cliché of film portraits of writers), a return – via a shot of the intercom – to his cheap hotel room where he orders a cheese sandwich and a glass of milk *en francais*, then with friends consulting the *I Ching*, photos of Greece and his Norwegian girlfriend, Marianne, a segue to some Greek stores in Montreal and Cohen's distaste for meat ("Here was the Market," *Parasites of Heaven* 54), back for *un verre de lait* and *un sandwich au fromage*, then a public reading in a university setting, and finally at a small party with friends, playing a guitar and singing "Twelve O'clock Chant" (*Spice-Box* 20). Overall, this heavily edited section of *Ladies and Gentlemen, Mr. Leonard Cohen* lacks the sustained performative values to be found elsewhere in the documentary. Even if the montage parallels Cohen's assemblage of self, the result feels bitty and inadequate – like this essay? – straining to avoid dullness?

An effortfulness also pervades the gathering with Cohen's friends who are clearly uncomfortable with the camera's presence. Without Cohen's cool, they cannot pretend the lens is not there; instead, they try to perform convincingly their difficult role of having a relaxed time. As with many New Year's Eve celebrations, where there is a not-so-subtle anxiety about having a fabulous time, their acting out of near-euphoria fails. This long scene is also awkward because Cohen's voice-over now sounds falsely oracular, given the post-Feminist sensibilities of today's viewers: "Sexuality is general, and although only one man may be receiving the favours of a woman, all men in her presence are warmed, and that is the great generosity of women." While these sentiments foretell some of the positive, communitarian impulses of the later 1960's, the gratitude expressed has a note of condescension rare in Cohen. The camera signals the end of the party by a close-up of a pair of shoes, then tilts upwards to reveal Cohen, alone, playing on a harmonica, which leads into his v.o. reading of perhaps the best love lyric ever written in Canada: "As the Mist Leaves No Scar." This is the poem that Irving Layton chose to open the vibrant (seminal?) 1962 anthology, *Love Where the Nights Are Long: Canadian Love Poems*, with erotic drawings by Harold Town.

Using disjunction as continuity, the editor cuts from the private evening among friends to a crowded, academic party. The anonymous narrator quotes Cohen as saying, "Poetry is not an occupation but a verdict," and the voice-over sketches in with still photos Cohen's involvement at McGill as a fraternity president "who fought to retain its exclusive Jewish nature."

At this statement, the documentary cuts to a shot of Cohen laughing: "I don't like the way the evidence is building up. I've got Westmount, I've got the chauffeur, I've got the fraternity, I've got the politics." Ignoring an interruption from the interviewer, he presses on towards the punchline: "all I have to tell you now I was good in sports, and I've completely ruined the cliché of the poet forever." With this exchange, an overt Bakhtinian dialogic has entered the film: the god-like authority of the unidentified voice-over is subtly disputed. The subject in front of the camera intervenes as a joint filmmaker – and biography mutates towards autobiography. As in *Don Quixote*, the character's awareness of the self-image projected in the earlier portion makes for a less naïve, more self-conscious understanding in the second part.

From this jesting, Barrie Howells, the editor, cuts to a dark street scene where Cohen wanders about, looking into store windows at various ads, magazines, and tabloids. His voice on the sound track is heard reading from "The Genius," a stark poem of history and protest: "For you/I will be a ghetto jew" (*Spice-Box* 78-9).

The mood shifts again with Cohen on stage in front of an appreciative audience, doing a comic shtick: "I mean you're very concerned with unwanted babies, but nobody cares for unwanted hair." The wit of his comic bathos brings popular culture into juxtaposition with social and political issues, creating a post-modern style, one of irreverent awareness. By flouting the boundaries between the serious and the absurd, Cohen makes laughter carnivalesque, subversive, freedom-giving, and dialogic: "Laughter demolishes fear and piety before an object, before a world, making of it an object of familiar contact and thus clearing the ground for an absolutely free investigation of it" (Bakhtin 23).

To the audio sound of the audience's laughter, the NFB film cuts to Ben's delicatessen late at night, where, according to Cohen, "is drawn this very urgent cross-section of people who have somehow committed the very first rebellious act that a man can perform, refusing to sleep."

The next scene is back at the hotel, with images of Cohen writing to music heard on the sound track, overlaid with excerpts in his voice from several poems, such as "I am with the hunters/ […] /and I am with the hunted" ("On Hearing a Name Long Unspoken," *Flowers for Hitler* (25). He re-phrases his divided self in an account of how in 1961 he anticipated the Bay of Pigs invasion and went to Cuba: "I wanted to kill or be killed." At a public reading, this ambivalence is further displayed – and has become familiar enough to viewers to aid in cinematic transition when Cohen asserts that he was there "fighting on both sides." According to Bakhtin, "true seriousness is the destruction of all false seriousness" (Bakhtin 312), and the audience is delighted with Cohen's insightful, amusing, schizoid performance piece about Canada – which is more comic monologue than poetry – "The Only Tourist in Havana Turns His Thoughts Homeward" (*Flowers* 38-9).

At its apparent conclusion, *Ladies and Gentlemen, Mr. Leonard Cohen* cuts to Cohen strolling through a Montreal arcade, gazing at a toy bandbox of musicians. In this pseudo-epiphany – with its implied closure of self-recognition – there is a close-up of a drummer, then of a swaying trumpeter blowing his horn, and finally of Cohen himself taking aim with a rifle at a shooting gallery as his off-camera voice reads his sardonic, brilliant, comically affirmative poem, "The Music Crept by Us" (*Stranger Music* 58), whose title playfully alludes to T.S. Eliot's *The Waste Land* (l. 257).

Having watched until the "end" of the film, the first-time viewer is now surprised to see a countdown of large numbers, both numeric and written – something that typically *precedes* a film. The anonymous narrator announces that at "the completion of the shooting of this film, Cohen was invited to a screening room to take a look at himself." We begin watching Cohen watching what we've just watched. He notes that

> "[t]his is a very privileged thing to be able to see yourself sleeping. I think it's an experience very few people have."
>
> "That's right."
>
> "But of course the fraud is that I'm not really sleeping."
>
> "It's a very privileged thing to see yourself pretending to sleep."
>
> "Yes, I think that's even more, a privilege of a higher and more esoteric order, because there are some people who are very very interested to know how they look when they are pretending."

This discussion of acting segues into further performance. The viewer watches Cohen get out of the hotel bed again and go to the window to raise the blinds – only this time he does so maladroitly and they fall at an awkward diagonal: "I was always good with my hands." His self-deprecating humour is part of his charm of vulnerability, but the innocent viewer is puzzled by this duplicity since visually documented reality is now being re-imaged and revised. Earlier, Cohen had been shown smoothly raising blind, but this reinserted out-take makes visible an omitted and contradictory shot, revealing selectivity and staging in violation of the basic premise of the genre: the recording of reality. Paradoxically, this exposure of a created persona lends credibility to both the filmmakers and their subject. By undermining the perceived truth of the on-screen biography, the directors invite trust and empathy though an honesty of understanding that involves deconstructing images. A parallelism can be found in Cohen's songs, where sincerity mixes with self-mockery, and, via the second person pronoun, "you," he invites listeners to share a meta-awareness that is savvy about the inauthentic.

The editor then cuts to a shot of the intercom speaker, which is in a different location, since the camera pulls back to reveal the poet in a bathtub. As we listen to Cohen's commentary, we realise we're watching an out-take, an experimental oddity back then:

> This is a situation for whatever the reason a man has allowed a number of strangers into his bathroom. Now it's true we're [first person collective!] making a film about my life and the film purports to examine my life closely and the bath is part of my life, but still regardless of the reason, here in 1964, a man has invited a group of strangers to observe him cleaning his body.

The footage shows Cohen writing on a notepad in a white porcelain tub as a second Cohen imaged in the screening room is prompted to share his impressions of himself, providing us with further exegesis and confession through deconstructive "takes" on the process of his self-portraiture:

> "You must find this interesting."
>
> "I find it very interesting. I find it – I find it sinister and, of course, I find it flattering because there is a point where every man shares the Agha Khan's delight at selling his bathwater."

Cohen, still in the tub, stops writing in his notebook and begins to draw on the bathroom wall in large block letters:

> "CAVEAT EMPTOR."
>
> "What did you mean by that inscription? A message to the audience?"
>
> "Yes. Caveat emptor. Let the buyer beware. I think… I think that I had to for a moment act as a double agent for both the filmmakers and the public. I had to warn the public that… this is not entirely devoid of the con."
>
> "C.O.N."
>
> "Right."

Cohen has iconoclastically broken his own self-created film persona, but in the act of doing so he is able to project a more sophisticated, more "honest" and complex performance of self.

The final cut is to an exterior scene, with Cohen on Montreal's wintry sidewalk, wiping his nose repeatedly, an intensification of the gesture in the opening monologue. The narrator's summarising voice-over is prophetic: "So it is time to go, back to Greece and the girl and the sun, and always back to the work, for as Leonard Cohen says, 'there are dreams of glory whispering through the wires of his spine.'"

Ladies and Gentlemen, Mr. Leonard Cohen, we now know, not only represents that fantasy, but also helped it come true.

But why am I writing this montage of bits and pieces when I have a novel to revise that's due out in the spring?

Because, back in a boxed-in time, the CBC telecast of this celluloid life imaged an exhilarating freedom. Cohen's funny, eloquent self-concern floated free of what Northrop Frye labelled a "garrison mentality." Narcissus, I knew, had been punished for looking too long and longingly at his own reflection, but here was this guy playing around and being fascinated with his own camera images as he usurped the directors' job, and staged himself for the lens with insight and humour – and he was being rewarded with fun and fame! In Cohen's refusal to be passively portrayed and in his giving expressive shape to a protean self, *Ladies and Gentlemen, Mr. Leonard Cohen* offered a funhouse mirror that also doubled as a kind of window.

Having halted me in front of a television set for 44 minutes and 1 second, Cohen agilely stepped away, and in the glassy grey mirror now suddenly blank, I could glimpse possibilities of my own shifting, multiple, un-Canadian self about to be introduced.

The sense of the fictive being unavoidably part of the truth of human yearning permeates Cohen's lyrics, and underlies their tone of amused melancholy. In apparent fulfilment of the narrator's voice-over prophecy at the end of *Ladies and Gentlemen*, Cohen has become a pop icon. In 1966, a year after the NFB film was released, he "realized he couldn't earn a decent living as a writer," and spoke of his intention to "become the Canadian [Bob] Dylan" (Nadel 141). His first album was released late in Canada's centennial year, 1967, and the man who in this film has tipped us off to the con game being played out via mediated images with his warning of buyer beware, became a commercial performer. Yet, I would argue, his career has had a complex, ironic, awkward, graceful double agency that makes him culturally Canadian. In 2008, four decades after *Songs of Leonard Cohen*, he was inducted into The Rock and Roll Hall of Fame: "not a distinction I coveted," he says (Lepage

B3). Though now an official icon, Leonard Cohen remains – as this early film self-portrait suggests – wary of iconicity.

In mingling documentary genres, *Ladies and Gentlemen* is both traditional and iconoclastic, emerging, like Cohen, during Canada's "identity crisis." In this confused and fertile period, colonial, modernist, and postmodern sensibilities coexisted in Canada, and were reflected in the language and the narrative form of three novels of that era: the fairly traditional prose and structure of Hugh MacLennan's *The Watch that Ends the Night* (1959), the elliptical and imagistic writing of Sheila Watson in *Double Hook* (1959) – her prose version of *The Waste Land* transposed to the interior of British Columbia – and Cohen's own iconoclastic, very self-aware, and phantasmagoric vision of Québec's culture and politics, past and future, in *Beautiful Losers* (1966a). It is appropriate then that this NFB film, in an encyclopaedic act of hybridity, contains all six of the documentary genres that Nichols identifies. Reflective of the clash of attitudes, tones, and values during the era of its making, *Ladies and Gentlemen, Mr. Leonard Cohen* manages to register the contradictions and ambivalences of both a poet and a nation at a time of shared emergence.

CHAPTER 4

Ghosts, Leaves, Photographs, and Memory: Seeing and Remembering Photographically in Daphne Marlatt's *Taken*

Frances SPROUT

Vancouver Island University, BC, Canada

Daphne Marlatt's novel *Taken* belongs to a sizeable body of Canadian literature for which the photograph is an important trope; Russell McDougall even calls Canadian writing "compulsively photographic" (1987: 112). Generally, this Canadian literary recourse to the photograph either exploits the access it provides to the past or challenges photography's positivist and exclusivist claims to representation.[1] Many well-known Canadian novels – among them Joy Kogawa's *Obasan*, Thomas King's *Medicine River*, Timothy Findley's *The Piano Man's Daughter* – do both, as does *Taken*. Their narrators' memories of the past are prompted by photographs, but these narrators also remember what the photographs fail to represent. *Taken* similarly explores the elements involved in knowing, remembering, and memorialising, but with a difference. Rather than simply using photographs as a conduit to the past or using photographs to demonstrate the problems inherent in memory and representation, *Taken* uses the photographic process itself – the photochemical play between

1 Besides McDougall, Linda Hutcheon and Lorraine York, among others, have responded to Canadian writers' use of the photograph. York summarizes "the functions of photography in contemporary Canadian literature [. . .] as an analogue to memory and the fictional process, as a reminder of the past, as a haunting image of death or loss of identity, sometimes as an image of cultural continuity in the fragile but enduring human chain" (1988: 165). I would add that the photograph also often functions as an analogue for that which is always frustratingly beyond language as well as to emphasize the politics of representation. Indeed, these additions are suggested by York's observation, in regards to Alice Munro's writing that, "like the iconic photograph, the past – and all its levels of meaning – defeats us" (41).

light and dark, positive and negative – to suggest more inclusive ways of knowing and remembering.

Marlatt's novel achieves this in three ways. First, structurally and stylistically, *Taken* evokes the photochemical process as much as the photographic product, foregrounding darkness and, concomitantly, unknowing as productive elements of representation. Negative and positive are emphasised as part of a continuum, rather than as diametrically opposed. Second, the novel emphasises vegetation as another form of photo-graphy, of light-writing, thus exploiting indirectly an extensive body of work which reads the photograph as oscillating "between technology and magic" (Benjamin 1980). This expanded view of the photographic troubles its documentary and positivist associations; as well, it reminds us of the photograph's identification, since its earliest appearances, with the ghostly. Thus it overlaps the novel's third approach to a renewed understanding of the photographic as a technology of memory. By exploiting the hauntedness which countless theorists have read as central to the photograph's ontology, Marlatt supplements the camera's representation with ghosts which gesture beyond the frame.

Marlatt's triple approach to seeing photographically is announced in the novel's opening words: "ghost leaves [which] come up in the half-light, translating themselves from misty grey to yellow" (1996: 3). Here ghostly vegetation writes with light, evoking the photochemical process of development from negative to positive. Structurally and stylistically, *Taken* continues to evoke this process and to associate it with the value of liminal and contingent knowledge. Thus the various interwoven narratives gradually coalesce to form a cohesive picture just as a positive image emerges in a darkroom; the reader's dawning comprehension of the relationship between the novel's opaque and indeterminate various narratives parallels the visual translation of the ghost leaves, which themselves suggest the development of a photograph.

For example, although the first-person narrator is unidentified, we can situate her in some "November" in a "space through which those leaves glimmer, alder and fern in the wet earth" (3). These leaves link the narrator to an unidentified "she" who "begins to coalesce somewhere behind my eyes, behind the hand over my mouth," and we learn that there "were ferns where *she* was in the Blue Mountains of Australia" (3; my emphasis). From one paragraph to the next we shift from first- to third-person narrative and from present to past tense. More specifically, the novel's second paragraph situates its subject, whose identity and relationship to the narrator is still not clear, during a "War time." Again, the developing process is invoked in the description of the military background. Thus war is signified by "black and white time, whole cultures reduced to dirty adjectives under the acrid developer of national will" (3).

Compared to the lyrical description of the leaves that the gentle morning light allows to "translate themselves," this description of war decries the harsh reductive qualities of the "black and white." Coupled with the reference to the "acrid developer of national will," this description indicts the photographic apparatus as co-opted by national media representations of war. As well, the other common currency of "black and white" is its reference to epistemological systems that permit or acknowledge no middle ground. And of course a system by which an entire nation or culture can become the black in absolute opposition to another nation or culture's white allows and justifies the horrors of war, horrors that might be less acceptable should both groups see themselves overlapping in greys.

The evocation of the photochemical process in these two opening paragraphs points to two representational systems. One system allows vegetation to represent a specific place, signalling it by the glimmer of its leaves; the leaves also represent and even "translate themselves." Green by virtue of chlorophyll, they attain their infinitely variable shading through another conspiracy with light. The second system of representation comprises conventional photography as used in both family albums and media representation of world events. Although also capable of much variation between the poles of negative and positive, dark and light, this system is generally associated with a more reductive epistemology, as suggested by the connotations of the cliché "black and white." The contrasting descriptions of these two systems mark one of the novel's primary concerns: how to create a narrative that provides a readable and cohesive positive print without occluding all that a negative might indicate – most particularly the value of the darkness and the not- or the just- barely seen.

Although negatives can be read, they are generally associated with darkness and indeterminacy. The narrator's reference to the nighttime "depth of not-seeing before light begins to silhouette shapes we can identify" (7) proposes their value. Her comment that "[a]t night we could be anywhere" suggests the loss of possibilities which accompany a move into light and expanded visibility. This move leads to a signifying system that makes identification easier, but in which the surrounding visual materiality prevails over imagination, insisting on our locatedness in the here and now. The darkness offers more oneiric possibilities; it holds the "unremembered dream" from which the narrator startles, "losing indolent edges, my body's warm uncurling float in tropical seas" (7). Thus it connects the narrator to her tropical past, and also, through the suggestion of the amniotic, with her mother.

Nor is the darkness associated only with the narrator Suzanne's oneiric past. As she drives her lover, Lori, to the ferry, the headlights of the car pick out two deer "who stare across the road at a smaller movement disappearing," a movement which may or may not have been made by "the tail end of a cat" (19). As the car continues, "dark closes in beyond us, tree walls of dark enfolding a world cats and other creatures inhabit" (19). The light that illuminates the animals fails to provide a clear understanding of what it discloses. Further, the dark that closes behind the car demarcates a border between Suzanne's world and that which "other creatures inhabit." As it "enfolds" this world, the darkness veils it from a world that only sees the illuminated. At the same time, the word "enfolds" establishes darkness as protective rather than menacing.

Besides these direct references, *Taken* alludes to darkness consistently through narrative strategies that situate the reader in the half-light of transitional knowledge – knowledge that is incomplete, contingent on context or information either withheld or unavailable. This insistence on the impossibility of knowing completely, and on the concomitant possibilities offered by the darkness of incomplete knowledge, is explored through the photographic trope. The opening contrast between the developing and the reductively black and white is followed by pages that situate a protagonist named Esme somewhere in the British colonial Pacific "trapped in transit by the Japanese invasion of Malaya" (4). This Esme, whose relationship to the narrator is not yet clear, contemplates the photo of a man identified only by his absence that she "feels […] opening like a void she has failed to prepare for" (4). His arm, then his elbow, materialise, and he is transformed into "a man who adores her" (4). Gradually his worried expression appears, then his sports jacket and tie, and finally a name, Charles. Thus the description of a character mimics the photochemical process as the apparent void of the film's surface gradually reveals a visual image.

Just as the resolved image of a photograph requires interpretation, so Charles' image must be contextualised. The narrative advises that this snapshot was taken as Charles and Esme were on their way to celebrate the news of her pregnancy; that, by a "stroke of luck," they had "been on leave in Australia to visit her parents […] when Malaya was invaded"; and that Charles has since decided to "go back – to do his duty" (6). Ironically, just as we begin to feel "in the picture," the picture itself is revealed as a flawed or incomplete representation, dependent on the narrative for further contextualisation. The documentary clarity of the photograph, we realise, discloses neither the pregnancy, nor Charles' imminent departure. The narrative details that supplement the description of the image reveal the photograph's inadequacy in representing a past moment, a moment that conflates the personal and the more conventionally historical.

As her narrator, Suzanne, describes Charles' image, then, Marlatt sketches the binary by which a photograph is both exploited for the access it provides to the past *and* challenged for its limited representation of the past. But by evoking the process of development through her description of a gradually-materialising Charles, Suzanne also suggests other ways of seeing photographically. Indeed, her narrative implies that we can continue to "develop" photographic images either imaginatively, intuitively, or by relying on information from such sources as the family's oral history. In thus acknowledging what the portrait fails to represent, she simultaneously marks her own narrative as contingent and provisional, thus allowing the developing narrative to leave room for knowledges which have not yet been revealed.

The contingency and provisionality Suzanne makes room for in describing her father's portrait similarly marks her moves between other photographs that connect past and present. Indeed, indeterminacy governs the relationship between the interwoven narratives which challenge the reader to assemble their meanings, to allow a meaning to *develop*. The first two of these interwoven narratives generally conform to the pattern set on the opening page of a division into a third-person, past-tense narrative – primarily concerned with imagining and re-telling the story of Esme's wartime years as a young bride and mother – and a first-person, present-tense narrative in which Esme's daughter, Suzanne, confronts her lover's departure and meditates on the role family history plays in that relationship. The boundaries between the two narratives, however, quickly begin to blur: in one early section, for example, the narrator muses, "i can almost touch her skin"; no transition is made between this and the following sentence with the confusing result that we assume that the speaker who can "almost touch her skin" is also the voice who complains that her eyelashes are "[m]ingy" (6). Only with a careful re-reading does this become clear, so that just as "she" only gradually "coalesces somewhere behind [the narrator's] eyes" on the opening page, so does this "she" gradually coalesce for the reader to become Esme, the narrator's mother. This identification is only indirectly confirmed when the narrator speaks of her father proposing to this woman we have watched resolve from "she" to "Esme" and, finally, to the narrator's mother.

While this slippage between first and third person contributes to the deliberate indeterminacy of the narrative, the comments and thoughts attributed to "her" can credibly be read as part of the narrator's own store of family memories. More difficult for the reader is that this slippage is often marked by a problematic assumption of omniscience that challenges any easy identification of first- and third- person. In one section, for example, the narrator wonders if "she f[ou]nd the nights quiet in Leura," and then imagines Esme reading a letter from her husband (8). In this letter, Charles writes that, while comfortable enough in his hotel, he is working so hard that he hasn't even time to enjoy a quiet *stengah*. This reference to the ritual of the social drink "explodes with its flash of associations," and the narrator proceeds to describe her mother having drinks at the Lone Pine Hotel (9). This description is then revealed as another invention, suggesting that "perhaps she was not really there at all but longing to be with him, imagining herself there in his hotel room" (11). Over the next few sentences this narrator and her metafictional musings seem to disappear, replaced by an omniscient rendition of her mother's "imagining [that] went that far, as far as herself in cheong sam […] hibiscus in her hair […] like some concubine's […] Isn't that what he would like?" (11).

The young bride supposedly speculates about "what all men liked" and then wishes that "she could have given herself […] just once, just once holding nothing back" (11). Such speculation is obviously too private ever to have been accessible to the daughter except by the sort of imaginative re-creation she performs here. Thus it blurs the borders between the first-person narrative and the third, simultaneously blurring the borders between the respective subjectivities of mother and daughter. These overlapping subjectivities mirror the shifting subjectivities invoked by the camera and its products, connoted, in the description above, by the reference to the photographic "flash of associations." The narrator's apparent ability to know her mother's thoughts recalls the comment by a character in Marlatt's earlier text *Ghost Works* that she wants to use her camera "to see, into them, into their hearts as if that might let her know them" (Marlatt 1993a: 10). Such a use of the camera clearly expands any understanding of the photographic as mechanistic and objective.

Rather than rendering the photographed person an object, Marlatt seems to suggest, photography can also facilitate exploring another subjectivity imaginatively. She also reminds us that, as Marianne Hirsch says,

> existing in time, the subject is also always temporally other, that is, always in addition to the present self, a previous or subsequent and anticipated self. By selecting one instant out of the subject's temporal existence, the photograph stages the subject's own specular self-encounter as an encounter with otherness: the subject represented in the photograph is always *other* to the one looking at the picture (1997: 89).

Prompted by a photographic record of one instant from her mother's temporal existence, *Taken*'s narrator imaginatively explores her mother's other potential selves, other unrecorded instants of her subjectivity. While the novel provides few instances of the narrator confronting an image of her own *other* in a photograph, the narrator's use of the third-person pronoun to refer to her childhood self denotes the same metaphysics of contingent, shifting subjectivity.

For the reader the effect of this othering of the narrator's childhood self, through the third-person pronoun, is, once again, to experience a gradual coalescence or development. While we may assume that the child Suzanne, introduced by name on page 79 as "[t]heir child [who] was born into a fragmented circle of refugee friends," must be the narrator's younger self, the choice of different pronouns to refer to adult and child defers *positive* confirmation of this knowledge until page 98. Simultaneously, of course, such deferral prolongs an exploitation of the possibilities allowed by the state of not knowing, the possibilities of the negative, while drawing attention to the multiplicity of selves the narrator explores while viewing the "album full of baby photos, grandparents and babies, Mummy or Daddy with babies" (95).

Confirmation of the child's identity for the reader, and integration of selves by the narrator, come through a repetition of a sentence which explicitly identifies the "i" of the first-person narrative with the young Suzanne: "So she would know where she lived" becomes "So i would know where i lived" (98). Significantly, this passage connecting the narrator with her earlier self and clarifying the reader's comprehension deals explicitly with the relationship between place and identity, thus highlighting a central interest of *Taken*'s – the role of place in representation and memorialisation. After the adult narrator integrates her childhood and adult selves through a change of pronouns, she remembers that her father taught her about place through stamp-collecting: "[s]o she would know where she lived, what she was (always with reservations) part of" (98).

Suzanne's narrative moves between pronouns – her easy slippage into first-person when offering her mother's imagined thoughts as well as her tendency to discuss her childhood self in the third person – mark an exploration of subjectivity across time, but equally draw attention to place. The changing pronouns mark movement between Suzanne on her British Columbian Gulf Island and her mother in Leura, imagining herself some*place* else. This movement links the place of the narrator's present and the Blue Mountains "where she was," so linking what we gradually recognise as daughter and mother, Northwest Pacific and Australia, present and past. The subsequent association, then, of changing pronouns with childhood geography lessons intensifies this emphasis on place and its role in understanding the past. I underline this focus on place because it pertains particularly to Marlatt's use of the photographic as a technology of memory.

Indeed, through Suzanne's exploration of place not only to know her present but also to understand her past, Marlatt suggests an antidote to what Paul Virilio calls "topographical amnesia" (Virilio 1998: 116). Or rather, she has Suzanne explore and exploit this amnesia, paradoxically, to restore memory by placing her personal and familial memories within the historical context of British colonialism, World War II, and that war's Japanese prisoner-of-war camps; through a confusion, if not a forgetting, of place, Suzanne insists on the relation between her family past in another part of the world and the immediate context of the Persian Gulf War of the late 20th century. Thus the amnesia which Virilio sees as negative allows Suzanne to know the past in more inclusive ways than allowed by previous technologies of memory.

To develop his claim of a prevailing cultural condition of topographical amnesia, Virilio outlines the fall through history of our relationship with space, the ways that we image, imagine, and, consequently, remember our place in the world. Thus he describes the Method of Loci that "Cicero and the ancient memory-theorists" used to "consolidate natural memory"; this was a "*topographical system* [...] an imagery-mnemonics which consisted of selecting a sequence of places, locations, that could easily be ordered in time and space." As Virilio describes it:

> you might imagine wandering through the house, choosing as loci various tables, a chair seen through a doorway, a windowsill, a mark on a wall. Next the material to be remembered is coded into discrete images and each of the images is inserted in the appropriate order into the various loci. To memorise a speech, you transform the main points into concrete images and mentally "place" each of the points in order at each successive locus. When it is time to deliver the speech, all you have to do is recall the parts of the house in order (110).

Virilio argues that the coupled traumas and technologies of the modern battlefield, augmented by the aural and visual technologies of the everyday, have disrupted our relationship to space to the point that we have arrived at a condition of "topographical amnesia" (116). We can no longer rely on stable, distinct *loci* to hold the concrete images capable of triggering memories; instead, the "fusion-confusion of eye and camera lens" has led to standardised "ways of seeing" which have reduced our "mnesic choice" (117-8).

Marlatt similarly indicts technology, linking it with the traumas of the battlefield, by having Suzanne mourn her mother's death and her lover's departure against the backdrop of the media representation of the Persian Gulf War. Suzanne's constant reference to place as she struggles with personal and familial memory illustrates aspects of topographical amnesia, echoing its disorienting and displacing effects. Although it occurs far away, the Gulf War has so invaded Suzanne's life as to be partially responsible for Lori's departure, the lovers having quarrelled for weeks over their responses to it. By formulating the Gulf War as a television serial that fills "the space around us [...] with controversy," she points precisely to the disrupted relationship with space that Virilio attributes to the various tele-technologies of the 20th century (Marlatt 1996: 81).

Not only does a technological representation of war fill the space around the lovers; even more, through a combination of tele-technology with the magic of optical illusions, "in [their] own kitchen hushed, listening to the news," they see themselves "figured in the window like apparitions on a TV screen" (81). In this spectral form, they are magically transposed to "Baghdad blowing up," and become images to accompany "[t]he sound of bombs, an excited journalist's voice describing the street from his hotel window" (81). This image of the lovers as apparitions imaging the war manifests the disrupted perception of space that concerns Virilio. For Suzanne, however, this disruption is potentially productive: it forces her to consider this relation between the war *there* and her life *here*, a West Coast island. Enclosed by a seemingly "tangible skin [of rain] around the house, she muses, a wet morning here and the war there in the late afternoon of the desert – they coexist" (37). By asserting this coexistence and attempting to understand it, she resists the media representation of the desert as a distant and objectified "tactician's dream" (38). Instead, she grapples with the tele-technologies of the media that bring the horrors of a far-off war into her bedroom and kitchen, confusing here and there, but that simultaneously and paradoxically maintain, through objectifying language, the distance they have collapsed.

While Suzanne resists the media representation, though, she does not simply reject the technology involved. Rather, she exploits the disruption of her normal, empirical relationship with space by tele-visual technology to explore ways of living ethically in a global community. This is exemplified in her reading of the optical illusion which turns herself and Lori into haunting images of a far-off war. By comparing their reflection in a darkened window to a television image, she challenges the media's attempt to represent the Baghdad bombing as distant. Instead, she represents herself and Lori as folded into the regularly-televised battle scenes where they are "historically accountable and furious at a complicity neither of us [want] to recognize" (81). This image of accountability and complicity destabilises the tele-visual technology's scientific base – and its attendant claims of documentary objectivity – by insinuating a comparison to magic, haunting, and the trickery of an optical illusion. The scientific ability to transport moving images from far-off wars is matched by the startling effect of an apparition that depends on the darkness outside as much as on the light within the room.

In insinuating a comparison between tele-visual technology and magic, Suzanne follows a path marked by Walter Benjamin who finds a relationship "between technology and magic" in photography's potential to "open up […] the physiognomic aspects of the world of images, which reside in the smallest details, clear and yet hidden enough to have found shelter in daydreams" (1980: 203). As well, Suzanne's recurrent references to vegetation recall the series of plant photos by Karl Blossfeldt in which Benjamin grounds his discussion of the camera's revelations.[2] But rather than meditate on photographs of plants, Suzanne discusses the vegetation directly. She presents the leaves themselves as images under photo-chemical development, speaking, in the already-cited example, of "ghost leaves […] translating themselves from misty grey to yellow" (3). Thus she reminds us that plants are another way of writing with light, and that, as Eduardo Cadava stresses, "There has never been a time without the photograph, without the residue and writing of light" (1992: 87). By depicting plants as representing place, writing it with light, she expands the possibilities for seeing photographically. The light-writing of plants – whether through photosynthesis or through the plant's transformation in different kinds of light – manifests itself throughout the novel: in the leaves and ferns of the opening pages, the ferns that mark the rock-faced cave of Suzanne's childhood dreams (95-6), the cedar and fir so characteristic of her temperate island home (7, 19), the branches she connects with words (21), the green surface of trees reflected on the green depth of the lake (104), the cedar plume that draws unreadable characters in the wind (129), and the cottonwood trees that launch their seeds onto a breeze on the final page. If these plants perform a version of photo-graphy, of light-writing, Suzanne allows us to see that what they are writing is place, that photo-graphy here becomes topo-graphy.

Suzanne's descriptions of leaves and ferns invoke the earliest recordings by the "pencil of nature" (Talbot 1969), recalling the many

---

2 After the sentence quoted in the previous paragraph, Benjamin goes on to say, "Thus Blossfeldt, with his astonishing photographs of plants, brought out the forms of ancient columns in horsetails, the bishop's staff in a bunch of flowers, totem poles in chestnut and acorn sprouts enlarged ten times, gothic tracery in teasel" (203).

theorists who characterise photography as moving between the two poles Benjamin speaks of: technology and magic. Thus she gestures to a tension long recognised as inherent to photography, even at its most "black and white." Once again, she works within the photographic to transcend its apparent limitations. By recourse to both the natural and the supernatural world, Suzanne exploits those complexities suggested by Geoffrey Batchen and André Bazin: Batchen points out that "the word *photography* itself," comprised of "two Greek components – *phos* (light) and *graphie* (writing, drawing, and delineation) – posits a paradoxical coalition of 'light' (sun, God, nature) and 'writing' (history, humankind, culture)" thus representing "an impossible binary opposition 'fixed' in uneasy conjunction only by the artifice of language" (1997: 101); Bazin characterises the photograph as "produc[ing] an image that is a reality of nature, namely, an hallucination that is also a fact" (1980: 243).

These complexities of the photograph rest on its ontological status as "this paradoxical image [...] that we read without disclaiming the notion that it retains something of the reality from which it was somehow released through its physiochemical makeup" (Damisch 1980: 288). As a "direct, physical emanation of the object, its luminous imprint" (Dubois 1995: 167), however, the photograph testifies as much to the absence as to the presence of the object that it signifies. Through this peculiar indexical relationship of the photograph with the object it represents – the "that-has-been" (Barthes) – the photograph has come to be closely associated with, even to symbolise, death. Not surprisingly, given the "magical value" which photography's "most exact technique" gives its images (Benjamin 202), this association has established the ghostly and haunted as a significant focus of photographic theory. The photographic image, as Philippe Dubois comments, is "haunted by the one intimate moment it had with a real that has vanished forever" (167).

Notably, the leaves through which Marlatt links the light-writing vegetation surrounding Suzanne with the photographs that help Suzanne remember her mother are "[g]host leaves" (1996: 3). Thus Marlatt's expansion of the photographic to comprise natural photo-graphy overlaps with her third approach to seeing beyond the positivist black and white. In this third approach, Suzanne exploits the hauntedness of her family photographs to transcend their limitations as positivist documents. Acknowledging the photographic as part of a technology which brings a distant war into her kitchen, she turns to the medium's magical dimensions to explore her relationship to a globalised space and a historicised past. The photo-graphic in vegetation allows her to emphasise photography as a photo-chemical process rather than simply as visual product; seeing it as a process allows her, in turn, to recognise the invisible in each representation. Simultaneously, she acknowledges the ghostly and the haunted to remind us of the absences these photographic presences signify.

The ghostly vegetation of the novel's opening offers a space for the imaginary, as implied in the "somewhere behind my eyes" where "she begins to coalesce" and also in the space at which either narrator or mother stares, the "space through which the leaves glimmer" (3). In both their ghostliness and their photographic sensitivity to light, these leaves signify and, at the same time, confound the borders between past and present, the dead and the living, the represented and the un-representable. Whether through the vegetation itself, or through its translation from darkness to light, from unseen to seen, the narrator is able to explore the presence of her mother "behind [her] eyes" and to see the entanglement of subjectivities that move her to other places she occupies, "not in the flesh" but through "the [haunting] memory-trace of it on [her] tongue" (7).

Suzanne's family photographs are implicated in a technology of memory that troubles her by its exclusions. She explicitly notes these exclusions in her observation that Esme paradoxically begins to "disappear from [Charles'] cine footage" just as "she has begun to show" as a mother (95). But instead of relying only on photographs to trigger her memory, Suzanne supplements them with her attention to vegetation and its response to light, its photo-graphy. This attention allows her to begin a ghostly re-visioning of her mother. It supports her desire to "jump that […] crevasse, between my eyes watching [the young Esme on film], my hands remembering the feel of black straw stiff with disuse, and her body there on the bed, brown deathspots already making their way to the surface of her skin" so that she can "go back to her body warm and cool in the wind off those rocks, her slightly embarrassed stance, eager to see herself as he saw her" (24). The movement from the dead maternal body makes of the younger celluloid version a kind of ghost, a re-animation of a dead loved one. This imaginary and imaginative movement also more fully animates the filmic record, allowing Suzanne to speculate about her mother's emotions; it exemplifies Suzanne's attention to the haunting possibilities of the photographic, particularly as manifest in the luminous and liminal transformations of the surrounding vegetation, even as these possibilities are linked to the photograph's concomitant limitations as documentary witness.

While the narrator looks at old photographs in an attempt to remember her mother, she notes that "[a]s the branches assume dim shapes in the half-light, there, really there outside in the dark, my connection fades" (21). This assumption of shape in the half-light recalls the darkroom development of photographs; here, though, the developing clarity of the image yields precedence to the shape-shifting possibilities of the process itself. Only in the liminal "limitless space" of dawn's transition from dark to light can she "open to her [mother's] presence in a way she never could when [her mother] was alive – or only in the very beginning perhaps" (21). Realising these possibilities, she tries "to write [her mother], reach her, bring her bodily out of the nothing, which is not nothing because she is there" (21). Again connecting the ghostly with the possibilities offered by transformative light, she says that what she is trying to recover is that "embalmed in [her] childhood," that which "[l]ike a ghost [...] goes on living alongside this reality" (120-1). That which haunts her also stimulates her to probe the family record with an openness to what this record fails to document.

In order to recover her mother, then, Suzanne supplements the family's documentary records and family history with the intuitive and the imaginative; simultaneously, she engages in a parallel recovery of her lover, Lori, in the wake of Lori's departure. Inventing other ways of tracing the past, she herself becomes ghostly, "haunting," as she says, "the evidence of what preoccupied you, books you left by our bed, fragmentary lists, telephone messages." As she goes through whatever fragments Lori has left behind, she decries the dangerous ramifications of remembering: "Not *memento*, not even *evidence*: those words won't do. It's the horror of knowing that, even as i remember in bits and pieces, i alter you into the ghost of someone you weren't" (121). So Suzanne is both ghostly herself and capable of turning her lover into a ghost. Examining the past means relying on technologies of memory that fragment and transform: Suzanne's difficult task is to haunt in a manner that not only satisfies her own needs but does so without transforming or destroying that which she remembers.

Horrified by the doubled ghostliness associated with the frustrating phenomenon of a memory which offers only "bits and pieces," Suzanne nonetheless tries to forge a productive technology of memory out of the very elements that frustrate her. The fragmentation of memory she observes prompts her to emphasise the provisionality of her own integrated narrative: "How," she asks, can she "put together a narrative of brightly coloured *bits* turned, turning as if to focus, and the falling patterns then. Beautiful forms. Illusions of continuity, of completion, made by mirrors" (26; my emphasis). Celebrating the beauty of "bits" provisionally integrated into an appearance of wholeness, she nonetheless warns against the seductions of the kaleidoscopic illusion. Even as her own narrative exposes the documentary failures of her family photographs, Suzanne cautions that her desire for a more inclusive family history will necessarily risk creating an "illusion of [...]

completion." To counter this illusion, she emphasises the provisionality of the narrative she assembles. By supplementing her descriptions of family photographs with references to the ghostly, she gestures to that left out of integrated family narratives. Just as importantly, though, her recognition of these haunting exclusions implies the inexhaustibility of meaning that any photograph holds.

References to the ghostly abound throughout the novel, but I find *Taken*'s most explicit and complex attempt to contend with the relationship between ghosts and photographs actually takes place in its margins. Here, the author's acknowledgements of other texts which haunt this novel include her reference to Tim Bowden's *Changi Photographer: George Aspinall's Record of Captivity* as one of her sources. This account of a young Australian soldier who spent several years in Japanese prisoner-of-war camps emphasises the contingency of what we visualise and memorialise culturally.

Aspinall was captured by the Japanese shortly after receiving a camera as a gift. His serendipitous choice of a folding Kodak allowed him more easily to hide the camera from his captors; the choice thus further demonstrates the role of chance in Aspinall's photographic record of his captivity. Despite the camera's lower detectability, however, Aspinall's subjects were still dictated by whether or not he could photograph them safely, and this often entailed finding a vantage point from which he could see without being seen. Already, then, every click of this captive's shutter represents, besides the image it records, a series of contingencies which limit and inflect the snapshots it is able to capture.

The emphasis on contingency extends to the other materials required by photography – film and developing chemicals. With limited film and no chemicals to prevent rapid deterioration in the tropical conditions, Aspinall fortuitously recognises developing fluid, fixative, and x-ray paper while unloading warehouse stores for his Japanese captors. Removing these supplies and hiding them in his camp carries a constant risk, not only of punishment, but also of an end to his attempts to document camp conditions. Further, taking and developing photographs with these materials depends entirely on experimentation; with neither timer nor thermometer, Aspinall's early efforts were, in his words, "basically hit and miss" (1985: 68).

Aspinall's photographs, which so clearly emphasise the contingency of photographic documentation, only hover at the novel's margins by virtue of Marlatt's acknowledgements. By so haunting the novel, they echo the narrative's concern with ghosts. The photographs are further resonant with the novel's trope of haunting in that they are buried to avoid discovery and destruction by the Japanese and dug up later to provide testimony at the Rabaul War Crimes Trials. While this disinterment suggests the snapshots' ghostliness, their return from the tomb to serve as evidence suggests that such haunting can be beneficial. Despite Suzanne's mistrust of "this [photographic] urge to fix an image so it won't fade over time" – she contrasts the "[p]ositives preserved in all their purity" with "what we actually experience – quicksilver, transient" (95) – Aspinall's photographs hover at the novel's margins to remind us that the fixed image can testify for the previously silenced and unseen. At the same time, however, by stressing difficulties surmounted to represent history, the narrative accompanying these photographs acknowledges their contingency and compellingly invites an exploration of knowledge(s) not yet illuminated by the camera's flash.

From outside the pages of *Taken*, then, the ghostly knowledge Aspinall offers insists on the relevance of the marginal to the more clearly central plot and characters. Throughout the novel, Suzanne's concern with hauntedness signals her desire to get beyond the material positivist representation of the past marked by photographs. Rather than reject photographs on the basis of their exclusivist version of history, however, Suzanne complements the knowledge they offer. She says of ghosts that they "have something to do with presence and absence, both" (104), inadvertently echoing what theorists of the photograph have noted about its ontology. Commenting that "what 'doesn't matter' comes back to haunt us" (113), she expands the photographs that document what supposedly matters in the family history to allow those haunting exclusions into her narrative. Thus she looks at a photograph of her mother as a teenage girl posed with her parents in front of their Malacca home, to see the unhappiness masked by the girl's new clothes. While the photograph testifies to an attractive and comfortable colonial lifestyle, Suzanne imaginatively retrieves memories of her mother's miserable exile to a London boarding school.

Suzanne troubles the photograph's claim of a privileged colonial lifestyle as she assumes Esme's subjectivity to remember her mother, in exile, missing her ayah rather than her own mother, Aylene. The gendered and class-conscious social demands of colonial life, not photographically documented for a family narrative, mean that Aylene played little part in raising her children, instead delegating their care to servants. These colonial social demands also shape the family record, obscuring any hint of the family's possible mixed-blood; they insist on the family claiming "Mother England" as home even though Esme experiences her time there as exile; and they confuse the family's perception of their relationship with the tropical island which serves as their home, but where they occupy a privileged position which marks them as outsiders.

As Suzanne notes, remembering on her temperate island the haunting smells, tastes, sounds and sights of her family's tropical life, "Ghosts are those who occupy a place, but not in the flesh, those who are left with only the memory-trace of it on their tongues" (7). Once again, she formulates a description of ghosts that is intricately ambivalent – not only do ghosts occupy a place in her formulation, but a place also haunts, in the ghostly form of words, still tracing itself on her tongue many decades after she has left it. Ghosts both occupy and remember place, and, for Suzanne, they advocate a memory that examines her relationship with place to insist that family history be understood in broader historico-political terms. In other words, they argue for, or perform, a topographical memory, offering an alternative to Virilio's topographical amnesia. But the topographical memory advocated by the ghostly differs significantly from the topographical memory offered by the classical Method of Loci Virilio looks back to. Central to this difference between a place-based memory as Suzanne develops it and the technology developed by classical rhetoricians is Suzanne's refusal of an epistemology that distinguishes between the material and the immaterial. By allowing the places she remembers to be haunted by the immaterial, Suzanne works to include that which other narratives and documentary records have excluded. Answering her grandmother retroactively, on her mother's behalf, she insists that "what 'doesn't matter,' [...] comes back to haunt us" (113). Her reflection of the "assumptions the daily is grounded on, housed in" further asserts the imbrication of the material and the immaterial through her use of the concrete, solid verbs – "grounded" and "housed" – that solidify assumptions, often dismissed as irrelevant (113).

As well, by thus "housing" that which supposedly does not matter, Suzanne indirectly invokes the architecture that supported the technology of classical memory. Elsewhere she suggests that this architecture, particularly in its most domestic manifestations, is already potentially undermined by the supposedly immaterial. "House" and "home" are, admittedly, not synonymous. Still, Suzanne's reference to "home, the impossible place" associated with "the blurred ideal each of us carries" at least muddies the mental image of a house through which one might walk, recovering detached objects in an organised and linear fashion (96). And if the mental image of a house provides the matrix for the classical approach to memory, Suzanne's etymological play throughout the novel – she plays, for example, the different connotations of "matter" against "mater" – broadens the notion of place as matrix for memory to include material and immaterial and to make room for the unconscious alongside the conscious.

Suzanne's insistence that the ghostly and the immaterial are crucial to understanding the past reflects Marlatt's desire to get to that which "[w]e can't consciously remember [but which is] there in our unconscious [...] in all the repressed babble, the language that just ripples and flows – and it isn't concerned with making sense" (Marlatt "When We" 1993b: 185). Suzanne's consequent refusal to separate the material from the immaterial, subject from object, body from landscape, leads her to supplement the photographic as a prompt to memory with attention to the light-writing of vegetation as well as with a willingness to haunt and be haunted. By refusing an epistemology that demands such separation, she begins a ghostly re-visioning of the disappearing woman who is/was her mother. Simultaneously, she revises the Method of Loci. This classical technique of places and images relied on a clear and exact correspondence between the visualised image and the memorised words it recalled. Suzanne's memories, however, are much more web-like, with one image often triggering several memories whose relationship she must then determine. The Method of Loci clearly separated the remembering subject, who walked through the visualised building, from the objects s/he recovered. Suzanne, instead, allows her subjectivity to dissolve in her memories, as manifest in the constant slippage between pronouns. Finally, the classical technique relied on a linearity that moved the remembering subject through the building from room to room, recovering words in the order necessary to the required rhetorical performance. Suzanne's technique is a circular and, ultimately, indeterminate one.

Developing her own method of loci, of relying on place as an aid to memory, Suzanne admits that place may be occupied by ghosts that influence memory in unpredictable, perhaps even un-knowable, ways. By associating ghostly memory with imagery of vegetation that changes its appearance, photo-graphically, with different light conditions, she roots, or grounds, these ghostly emanations to make them visible. At the same time, by emphasising the contingency of vegetation's visibility on light, she attempts to transcend the problematic and exclusivist aspects of the systems of representation and memory that she is interrogating, those systems in which the photograph is often implicated.

Thus while she recognises the exclusions of the family photograph collection and the role of the photographic in representations of war, Suzanne's attention to hauntedness and vegetative light-writing alerts us to other ways of seeing photographically. She speaks of the light of dawn before "things [...] harden into the clarity of the everyday, of separate categories, dissociated," contrasting it with the light of noon when "we pull in our senses [...] and limit ourselves to what we select of the visible" (116). In mourning her mother, she also "[m]ourn[s] the loss of early light which opens first to sound or smell or touch, not sight" and "the loss of being before knowing narrowed into the dangerously exclusive we label meaningful, or what counts" (116). While mourning, then, she comes to value those times when "[t]he eye, unfocused, gazes at water, air, all that envelops us, pre-dates us. Post-dates us too" (116). Through this unfocused eye, she declares herself part of the landscape, rather than its mastering observer.

In this landscape where "everywhere micro-factories of light combin[e] photo-chemical cells" (104), Suzanne sees place being written and remembered photographically while "something keeps inventing itself"; admittedly, this writing is "[w]ispy and silhouette-clear as a cedar plume drawing unreadable characters in the wind against that grey, that light nothingness" (129). A diffused and organic writing which refuses any separation of subject and object is not easily read: "There was always something and nothing, it just wasn't clear how they turn in the wind. How they might even be the same" (129). For Suzanne, though, this difficulty is valuable, confirming for her the intimate relationship between "something and nothing," between what matters and what we dismiss as unimportant.

Suzanne finishes her narrative by imagining the cottonwood seeds, the "long cottony filaments launch[ing themselves] on a breeze spinning them into nests, the gullets of fish, sludgy eaves troughs we failed to clean, an unseasonal snow no camera will catch […]. They go on spinning out of eyeshot, snapshot, beyond the reach of evidence. The stories we invent and refuse to invent ourselves by, all unfinished" (130). As do the leaves and ferns of the opening pages, these seeds will connect one place and time with another, yet to be imagined. If the camera claims to catch an instant of linear time, the cottonwood seeds trace a cyclical time beyond the reach of any mastering eye or lens. By evoking them, Suzanne herself performs a cycle; as her image of the cottonwood seeds gestures to the future, it simultaneously returns readers to the leaves of the opening pages. This circular movement offers an alternative way of envisioning time and place to the visual epistemology most often associated with the photograph. To complement the limitations of the family photograph album and other positivist representations of history, Suzanne leads us toward a photographic vision comprising the photo-chemical process of development; the many ways that vegetation writes with and is written by light; and the spectral associations which have long haunted the photograph – through this vision, we see, remember, and memorialise the unseen.

CHAPTER 5

"The Angel Voices": Photography, Film and Point of View in Ann-Marie MacDonald's *Fall On Your Knees*

Ron BONHAM

Vancouver Island University, Canada

I

Over the last century, photography and film have had indelible impact on the "grammar" as well as the "ethics" of seeing (Sontag 1978: 3). The initial focus of these technological arts on the object, on what Ortega Y Gasset refers to as "putting us within what is outside," (1956: 116) has shifted increasingly toward not the object but the eye and thus "into vision itself, into the subject himself" (114). Clearly both object and eye are essential in the dialogic working of digital technologies; thus point of view, what lies within and behind the eye, has been increasingly privileged in the visual arts. Candida Rifkind defines this important shift in emphasis: "the truth of the image is in the expression of its meaning and not necessarily in the details it contains" (2002: 32). Hence, film and photography have become simultaneously media and projections of our psychic depths, the means "to pour out [...] what is within" (Ortega 116) as well as its fullest expression.

As exploration of the nature of image deepened over the last century, the emphasis has shifted from the primacy of objects towards what Ortega calls "a pretext for something else" (111). Ann-Marie MacDonald's *Fall on Your Knees* is fascinating to interpret in this context as the novel, in a framing statement located in the opening chapter "Silent Pictures," announces exploration of "the vivid gradations of light and shadow that make the picture" (1996: 1). The "something else" Ortega mentions is clearly the exploration of the trajectory of light which takes us back to the eye.

As MacDonald, a film and stage actress and dramatist as well as a novelist, clearly understands the magical role of light and shadow, she explores the experiences of seeing in the structure, style, and thematics of *Fall on Your Knees*. Both the saga of four generations of a family, the Pipers, and a canvas of the first half of 20th century Canadian history (1899-1953), the novel reveals history as an "elaboration of cinema" (Ortega 99) where reality is never fixed but is an image of movement. MacDonald has emphasised the novel's inception not in words but "early images" and her role as recorder/projector: "And it was almost like, I'm a camera…" ("Interview"). Critical to an understanding of the novel as well as to full engagement in the work is the role of point of view. MacDonald's novel is one that grips us and does not let go; we are implicated as the work insists on not only projecting different points of view throughout its unfolding but also eliciting points of view from us as readers.

The reading of MacDonald's novel, in fact, draws on the tension between photography as a means to achieve unity, continuity, and preservation of secrets, and film as a medium that enforces disunity, change, and revelation. Sontag makes the point that photography developed at the time when the family structure was first seriously challenged, and hence is "an elegiac art, a twilight art" (15). Thus photographs allow for a degree of aesthetic distance while functioning as "incitements to reverie" (16). Film has no such neatness and refuses to "make reality atomic" (23), as montage challenges the stillness, the anesthetising nature of photographic experience (for both the photograph and the vicarious eye).

What brings these two arts together for MacDonald in both their complementarity and their opposition is the emphasis on point of view. The elephant in the room here – so large that it may be overlooked – is the identity and role of MacDonald's narrator. In discovering her process of narration, the author had to begin with questions of seeing and sight: "*Who is watching this? Whose eyes am I behind?*" ("Interview"). A mercurial, elusive, almost trickster-like figure, the narrator appears at times to be Lily, the last survivor of the immediate Piper family, but, at other times, is clearly an omniscient voice, an editorial commentator, and even the voice of/for the reader. A hovering presence, the narrator is like the guardian angel of the novel – a figure frequently mentioned by the Piper sisters and a hidden reference in the novel's title in the "Fall on your knees/O, hear the angel voices" (from the carol "O Holy Night"). This guardian angel is the watcher, the cameraman who "introduces us" to what Walter Benjamin refers to as "unconscious optics" (1985: 690). For Benjamin, film offers a "thoroughgoing permeation of reality." Unlike the painter or photographer who "maintains in his work a natural distance from reality, the cameraman penetrates deeply into its web" (688). The narrator, like the audience members at silent films in their nascency, thus interrupts and even ruptures the apparent outside objectivity of the tale. Like the novel's heroine Frances, who is given to "speaking all the lines in the script before they come on the screen," (192) the narrator calls out to the characters for us: "*Hurry Frances*" (147); offers comfort: "Everything's going to be all right" (155); questions the characters: "What, Frances? Something." (293); and even coins delightful words: "disfigurine" for the broken "Old Fashioned Doll" (257). This narrational technique reflects and reveals the penetrating power and multivalency of point of view in the novel, a work which cannot be fully understood without acknowledging the framing strategies, metalanguage, and embedded assumptions of visual culture provided by image technologies (photography and film).

II

Fall on Your Knees has been recognised for its 19th century epic structure: a family saga and a broad, sweeping historical canvas. A novel full of event and revelation, it covers more than fifty years and four generations of a family which experiences birth, death, and a kind of rebirth. The novel's epigraph, from *Jane Eyre*, and frequent references to that "English canonical novel" (Somacarrera 2004: 56), have been explored in academic essays[1] which clearly identify the Gothic tradition's influence on MacDonald's text. Somacarrera argues that *Fall on Your Knees* is a "Canadian rewriting of an English canonical novel like *Jane Eyre*," but, as a work which deconstructs the Gothic tradition from a psychological perspective, a text "which implies the subversion of a canon" (56).

As a novel full of heightened drama, coincidence, hidden and repressed desires, seduction, entrapment and rape, *Fall on Your Knees* has the essential stuff of Gothic melodrama. James Piper, the patriarch, is hounded by his own demons of desire for his daughters and his fear of these desires. His exotic child-bride Materia lives on the borders of sanity and takes her own life by gassing herself in the oven. The eldest daughter Kathleen is raised as an exotic hothouse flower, a musical

---

1 Of particular interest for the reading of the novel in light of the Gothic tradition are: Jennifer Andrews "Rethinking the Relevance of Magic Realism for English-Canadian Literature: Reading Ann-Marie MacDonald's *Fall on Your Knees*" *Studies in Canadian Literature*, 24, 1 (1999), 1-19 and Katarzyna Rukszto, "Out of Bonds: Perverse Longings, Transgressive Desires and the Limits of Multiculturalism: A Reading of *Fall on Your Knees*" *International Journal of Canadian Studies*, 2 (2000), 17-34. And of course Pilar Somacarrera's article quoted herein.

prodigy who discovers her passion for illicit Black music in Harlem and for the body of another woman before being raped by her father and dying giving birth to his twin children. Mercedes, the "good one," is a straight-laced and repressed schoolmarm, guarding family secrets while trying to prove her younger "sister" Lily a saint and mortifying her own flesh by eating coal. Frances, the "bad one," is sexually molested by her father, takes up the lost life of entertaining men as a stripper in a decayed speakeasy, and seduces a Black man who impregnates her. Lily, child of James and his own daughter Kathleen, is trapped in her crippled body as a result of her infantile polio and as a replication of her mother's image until she effects her escape in her red shoes. Such details point out that MacDonald has imitated and even parodied the essence of Gothic melodrama in her novel, with supernatural, religious, and racial elements added for good measure. However, the heightened description of the characters' lives and identities and the nearly overwrought incidents and convergences also owe a great deal to the sentiment of photography and the rhythmic montage of silent film. This is made evident in the "Silent Pictures" title of the first chapter as well as the suggestive titles of other chapters (e.g. "Moving Pictures," "Cheap Women 'n Cheatin Men," and the novel's final chapter, "Sudden Light").

In fact, the cast of characters – especially the members of the Piper family – is introduced to us through "gradations of light and shadow" as we are simultaneously exhorted to "look" and "imagine." However, when we come to Frances, the novel's central character, suddenly "this one is a moving picture." The narrative voice even breaks in with "what are you doing, Frances?" as the novel frames its ongoing dialogue between photography and film as ways of seeing.

Ortega's discussion of "proximate" and "distant" vision usefully informs the role of photography and film in our lives and, by extension, in MacDonald's novel. For Ortega, proximate vision "dissociates, analyses, distinguishes – it is feudal" (112). Interestingly, Materia, the mother, is often seen as a dark creature: what initially attracts James is that "she has the darkest eyes he'd ever seen, wet with light" (12). Materia is meanwhile drawn to James' white blondness, reminiscent of the "china figurines of English aristocracy" (10). James, led by Materia to Wheeler's Photographer, "felt that the [wedding] photograph had made them one" (13). Hence the Piper children are progeny of light and dark,[2] the genesis and expression of photography and film.

2 In fact, throughout the novel, MacDonald pairs up light and dark, black and white, in her lovers: an echo of the light and dark composition of film and photography.

The attraction between James and Materia is all about vision and seeing (the chapter of their first meeting is called "His Left Eye"). The words "sight," "eyes," and "blind" come up over and over, culminating in the ecstatic "Song of Songs": "thou has ravished my heart with one of thine eyes." Proximate vision is closely allied with photography here as it is controlling and "organises the whole field of vision" (Ortega 101). Photography is particularly associated with Kathleen of "the tower chamber" (97) as it is her picture that James wants to take with him to war. Although James is heading off to Europe because of his unnatural, erotic attraction to his daughter, he cannot let go of his control. In photography, the "central object is a luminous hero" (Ortega 102), and this is Kathleen. However, while the picture is forming, "Materia's hand fractures into light, framing Kathleen's blur of hair" (80). Here is an essential omen of what is to come – a transgression of the control James imposes – since the flash of light comes from Materia's scissors which will later be used to perform the Caesarian on Kathleen, extricating James' babies from her dying body. Sontag makes the point that the voyeuristic control of photography is a "semblance of rape" (24), an observation apropos of MacDonald's novel in that James, in discovering Kathleen in bed with her Black lover Rose, rapes his daughter and takes her home, imprisoning her until she dies in childbirth. However, photography, with its apparently tactile, fixed point of view, paradoxically creates duality and distance. The object of sight, as Ortega suggests, recedes in proximate vision, and what appears as control and unity results in aesthetic and even human distance: "It is a view of the world which denies interconnectedness, continuity, but which confers on each moment the character of a mystery" (Sontag 23). Kathleen's one preserved photograph, hidden away in the copy of *Jane Eyre* and later in the attic trunk, is the agent which gives the lie to control. When the photograph appears on the piano, placed there by Mercedes, James sees it and lashes out at Frances, who takes the blame for placing it there, in one of the most violent episodes in the novel. This parallels Mercedes' placing the picture of Frances' son Anthony on the piano at the end of the novel. Frances dies not knowing that this son of hers survived, but Mercedes, in a gesture for forgiveness, then realises that she can no longer control the family secrets and the family story.

In contrast to proximate vision, distant vision is spectral, "half-unreal," (Ortega 103) and since the "field is homogeneous" (Ortega 102), there is less distance and less control. Especially with silent films, which are Frances' inspiration and her choice over "talkies," emphasis is on the rhythm of the montage. As the projected film image is evanescent, temporised in its showing, it requires, or at least invites, direct engagement. Paradoxically, the object of sight is nearer than in proximate vision; it "begins at our cornea," (Ortega 104) and eluding control, finds its own authenticity, rhythm, unity. Such is the fused life and identity of Frances, so unlike her sister Mercedes who is always struggling with what is "behind her eyes" (374) and who sees herself from outside: "I pictured myself and Frances eating cinnamon toast and drinking cocoa at the kitchen table [...]" (375). Because she inhabits and takes charge of her life, Frances is eventually able to feel "a familiar yet unnameably old feeling. One she hadn't known was ever hers to forget. Happiness" (398). Mercedes, on the other hand, "is why purgatory was invented" (388).

Frances' early attraction to film and her acceptance of Lillian Gish and, later, Louise Brooks as her model, reveal her intuited affinity with distant vision. Frances was, in fact, baptised in the Empire Theatre (1982: 64), the temple of "ecstatic darkness" (197) where she finds her religion. Notably "uncanny" in her ability to replicate the movement and expression of film stars, she has an intense relation to film evident in her ability to reproduce "all the lines in the script the second before they come on the screen" (197). To secure her job as entertainer at the speakeasy, Frances draws upon "a solo second-hand foxtrot picked up from the movie screen" and "quips in moving-picture parlance" (288). Indeed, Frances' precocious affinity with distant vision – with the quasi-unreal which realises truth as evolution, as movement – is most evident in her discovery "that one thing can look like another. That the facts of a situation don't necessarily indicate anything about the situation" (142). Because her life embodies distant vision, she is, intuitively, the challenge to James' control, the focus of his violent abuse, and an object of his sexual gratification. Yet Frances is also the one to whom he, in his search for absolution, ultimately confesses his rape of Kathleen and the fathering of her children. Frances' anarchic determination to achieve distant vision enables her to see beyond the "official version" of events. In bravely exploring and authenticating her point of view with film as her locus, she ultimately restores truth and renewal to her family.

III

The cinematic design of *Fall on Your Knees* is, in fact, critical to its expression of the fluidity of reality, not as "datum" but as the "image of a movement" (Ortega 99). This design, drawing primarily on cinematography and film editing techniques, engages the reader in the novel as direct witness since aesthetic distance is collapsed and the multi-focalising nature of reality is captured and realised through montage.

A dramatic instance of freeze-framing is evident in the scene where James witnesses the death of Kathleen and the birth of his twins: "The Soul, half in, half out of the tomb of her body, is in very good condition, the hair freshly combed, the nightgown spotless, the face expressionless – the first divine divestiture has taken place, she has sloughed off her personality like an old skin. She won't need it where she's going" (143-4). MacDonald's visual detail here, supported by the urgent syntax, captures the eternal moment, James' indelible picture as "Clouds hover. Somewhere within is God, waiting." For James, "this is not really a painting but a moment freeze-framed by James' eye, the supernatural elements, if present, are invisible" (144). This passage brilliantly evokes the shift from object to eye as the reader also assumes James' point of view, at the same time recognising that this image is one James will never be able to modify or escape.

Frances' dreams are frequently presented as film where the covert reality of Kathleen's death and her own childish and tragic baptising of Lily and Ambrose struggle to emerge in the free play of the unconscious:

> But tonight Frances awakens with her throat constricted in a silent scream – Mumma in the garden on the scarecrow stick, wearing the old fedora and one of her baggy flowered dresses all crusty down the front, and she's holding the steak-and-kidney pie scissors with a bit of pink gristle hanging off. But the worst part is she has no face. Mumma. Frances is determined not to watch to the end of this silent picture, in case it becomes a talkie (306).

The dream-film here plays the reality of Materia's performing the Caesarian surgery on Kathleen. However, by not watching the film through, Frances temporarily blocks out recognition of the violent birth and her bungled baptizing of the infants in the cold stream at the bottom of the garden, resulting in Ambrose drowning and Lily contracting poliomyelitis. This film will come back to her again.

A powerful use of jump-cutting is evident when the photograph of Kathleen stares out at James; time reverses and collapses as memory assaults the eye:

> Then he sees the photograph. The laughing, leaning-forward girl with the halo of hurry, "Daddy!" The house is behind her and you can just see Materia in the kitchen waving. Something bright in her hand. Flashed against the lens. James can hear Kathleen laughing at him, totally unafraid, nothing to be afraid of. Not like now in this room. Now is the dim past. Then was the shining present. He hears her laugh. He hears the water trickling in the creek and flash goes Materia's waving hand, although her face is barely visible. Kathleen is fourteen. You think you're safe. Until you see a picture like that. And then you'll know you'll always be a slave to the

> present because the present is more powerful than the past, no matter how long ago the present happened (260).

The brilliant sense of language here, the tenses shifting and reversing, and the revelation of the moving picture behind the still adds to the power of this passage. Furthermore, it functions with the rhythm of montage as memory is projected on the inner eye:

> If only he hadn't let her go so far from home. If only he had gone with her to New York. None of it would have happened. She never would have got pregnant. Not that I regret Lily. Lily is my consolation but my first girl... She'd be with me now. *Oho my darlin'.* The breath assaults James' lungs as he comes out of the black and white picture back into the room of living colour (260).

This point of view window on the event shows the dramatic switch from "he" to "I" and then back out to "James" like the jump-cutting in film from wide angle to close-up, from interior to exterior, often conventionalised in the dramatic shift between black and white and colour.

The novel employs many instances of rhythmic montage; one of the most effective is presented when Boutros, the bouncer at the speakeasy, is driving his father Jameel's vehicle and passes Leo Taylor's truck with Frances in the passenger seat. Frances has covered herself with fake blood to engineer her seduction of Leo, but Boutros, obsessed with Frances, immediately assumes that Leo has abused her:

> Up ahead comes Leo Taylor's truck. It whizzes past them on the land side of the Shore Road. The one-second aperture of his headlights has taken a picture for Boutros which is just now coming up in black and white through the film of his eyes. Frances in the cab, looking straight at him, her face a battered mess. Taylor at the wheel laughing at her (365).

Immediately, Boutros cries, Jameel laughs scornfully at him, and their vehicle "hurtles off the road, over the ruts and along the cliff at eighty till the terrain changes abruptly to silent air" (365). The entire pacing of this passage, the event unfolding in inevitable movement, and the language of cinema ("aperture," "picture," "black and white," "film,") capture the simultaneity of action. The ironic misperception of what is transpiring in Leo's vehicle brings us back to Frances' discovery "that one thing can look like another" (142).

Rhythmic editing is handled most dramatically in the scene where James severely beats Frances when she takes responsibility for Mercedes' action of placing Kathleen's one remaining photograph on the piano. In fact, MacDonald in this particular scene uses the language of musical composition to score the montage of the beating. It is horrifyingly effective:

> The upbeat grabs her neck till she's on point, the downbeat thrusts her back against the wall, two eighth-notes of head on wood, knuckles clatter incidentally. In the half-note rest he lights up her pale face with the blue wicks of his eyes, and the lyrics kick in *con spirito*. "What right have you, you have no right, no right to speak her name, who's the slut, tell me who's the slut!" The next two bars are like the first, then we're into the second movement, swing your partner from the wall into the work-bench, which catches her in the small of the back, grace note into stumble because she bounces, being young. *Staccato* across the face, then she expands her percussive range and becomes a silent tambourine (262-3).

The language and syntax enact the beating as an artistic expression and place the reader as witness to that rhythmic movement.

Fall on Your Knees is also replete with examples of parallel cutting where there is a shift in *mise en scène* to contemporaneous and parallel action. "Hegira," a key section of the novel, presents its fullest use. Here Kathleen's journal is intercut with her daughter Lily's journey so that the meaning of "hegira," a spiritual exodus or departure, applies to both mother and daughter. As Lily travels to New York, largely on foot, to find out about her mother Kathleen's life there, she is reading Kathleen's journal which Frances has given her. Kathleen's journal presents her discovery of her artistic self, her lesbian identity, her great love for Rose, and her "maiden voyage" to fame and fulfilment:

> O Diary. My loyal friend. There is love, there is music, there is no limit, there is work, there is the precious sense that this is the hour of grace when all things gather and distill to create the rest of my life. I don't believe in God, I believe in everything. And I am amazed at how blessed I am (536).

This sacramental vision of life becomes Lily's guide and the mother's truest gift to her daughter: "Lily knows where she is going, it is only necessary to keep to the coast. If she can see the ocean on her left she can't get lost" (598). The ocean here acts as both physical and spiritual locus as her mother leads her to her truth and her spiritual home.

The cinematic style of parallel cutting conveys sense of urgency to the drama of events; it allows us as readers to see and experience what is unfolding from different perspectives, witnessing the characters' investments in the events while freeing us to realise our own perspectives – our own points of view.

In fact, narrative replication of point of view (POV) "shooting" is the most common and recognisable cinematic technique employed throughout the novel. Often within the same paragraph – and even within the same sentence – the narrative frame shifts from an exterior, omniscient perspective to a single point of view. Thus, as James presides at the dinner table over his three daughters, we are both inside and outside the experience: "Eat. Chew, chew, chew, offer it up for the poor souls in purgatory. *Frances* has difficulty getting through a whole meal at the best of times – maybe if *I* smuggle the liver into *my* pockets bit by bite" (184 italics mine). Frances feels James' disapproval and the threat of "the back of his hand" while her father turns to Lily with generous approval: "*He* turns to Lily and tugs one of her braids. So like her mother, her mother's lovely mouth and perfect nose, her eyes. So like Kathleen but for the blight. This only makes her more precious to *me*" (188 italics mine). Later, we experience a similar shifting in point of view with Mercedes considering her love and esteem for her father: "*Mercedes* waits. Daddy has never mentioned his mother to anyone but *me*, now at this moment [...] and perhaps once long ago to Kathleen. Mercedes holds *her* breath, not to startle the moment" (209 italics mine). Passages like these make use of the quick editing and camera techniques of film to have the reader positioned both within and without the situations to complexify the experience and to counteract any reductionist approach to seeing humans as simply good or evil, honest or deceitful.

The most dramatic example of POV in MacDonald's novel, however, is the chapter entitled "The Official Version," a key part of the text which, through the ironic deconstruction of its title, conveys the multivalency of truth and the power of seeing. Fabricating a fiction in a family/community to ensure and protect belonging, membership "is an imperfect system but it's the prevailing one" (166). Initially, "those who breathe a word of the actual facts" are shunned, rejected, and "easily dismissed as liars" until "as years go by the facts are eroded and scattered by time" (166). Here MacDonald shows that POV is not only what one sees but also what one opts to see, where one will invest one's urge and need to believe.

"The Official Version" is divided or fractured into several sections, presenting differing angles of perception on the story of Kathleen's death and the birth of her twins. Officially, Kathleen, who "looked lovely [...] in white," died of influenza and her child Lily "is the offspring of its grandparents" (165). We then have Mahmoud's point of view as he blames his daughter Materia for her "stupidity," and James for his "vanity" for "exposing the girl and her gift to the world." For Mahmoud, this is "exactly prostitution," and Kathleen "wound up a tramp" (166). He then blames himself for being "merciful" to his "idiot daughter" and the "bastard Piper" (167) and thus disposes of the family for good. "The Rocking Chair" offers us Mercedes' view of James' sexual abuse of Frances. Mercedes awakens to find Frances gone from the room and discovers her sister "in the rocking chair with Daddy" so "it's all right." Mercedes then displaces her upset at what she has witnessed:

> Back in bed Frances cuddled once more at her side, Mercedes starts to feel afraid. And a bit sick to her stomach although she can't understand why. She rises, goes over to the wash-basin and throws up. It must have been that smell of kidneys cooking that got her upset (168).

The smell here is actually the odour of the death of Materia who put her head in the oven. Meanwhile, Mercedes represses what she has seen and it remains hidden behind her eyes for years – a source of her repressed, prudish, and judgemental personality. Only years later, when the memory resurfaces, can Mercedes acknowledge that "there never was a rocking-chair, in this room or any other. Just the pale green wingback" (374). Clearly, as self-protection, she has opted for an invented point of view.

"The First Holy Sacrament" presents James' and Mercedes' points of view on the rescue of Lily from death and especially from the "devil – necessary evil." James and Mercedes share the same moral high ground and militancy against evil. James "just knows she's [Frances is] bad" (169) and that "there are no accidents, only tests" (170). Meanwhile, "at the age of almost seven," Mercedes defines herself as the "mother now" and "assumes responsibility for the soul of Lily Piper" (171). This understanding of James' and Mercedes' control of and pressure on Lily to be a model and ultimately even a saint leads to Lily's need to escape the family, an action effected by Frances.

"Babes in the Wood" presents Frances' point of view on the burden of guilt and sense of her own unacceptableness: "Daddy called her Lily because of something I did, thought Frances. It's to remind me of something" (172). Meanwhile she claims it is a good thing that Materia died "because if Mumma were here, she would know what a bad girl I've been" (174). At this time, Frances must strike out on her own as the rebel and bad girl in order to survive: "Frances never cried for Mumma after that night" (174).

In the last section of this chapter, "Lily Who Lived," the sisters' different assessments of Lily and the ways in which they will influence her self perception in turn are effectively summarised in contrasting points of view: "I am holding a miracle, thinks Mercedes. There is something wrong with her, says Frances under her breath" (175). Clearly, MacDonald's use of point of view editing and framing conveys the complexity, fluidity, and variability of reality – the "multiple fragments which are assembled" by the cameraman/narrator "under a new law" (Benjamin 688) not evident in the photograph.

Thus, the filmic devices and techniques used throughout the novel really emphasise the eye, not the object – the reality which is not "datum" but "the evolution formed when […] materials melt and fluidify" (Ortega 99). The ways of seeing in the novel are its essential element in unfolding the story of the Piper family, but, more importantly, draw the readers to an implication in the "ethics of seeing" (Sontag 3) as we realise the moral responsibility that must inevitably be taken up in the shaping of reality.

IV

Kathleen's vision and even her survival in the family narrative in *Fall on Your Knees* are associated with photography and the camera eye. This camera eye view is made clearest in her journals where she claims that "[e]verything in New York is a photograph" (466) and she would be the camera eye:

> I wish I could be invisible. Or at least I wish I didn't look like someone they [men] want to look at. They stop being part of the picture, they get up from their chess game and come out of the frame at me, blocking my view. What do they see when they look at me? (466)

Kathleen would be the pure "spectatorial" subject (Rifkind 31) if she had her choice so that she could absorb the full experience of New York. Ironically, she instead becomes the photographic object, "the photograph of a laughing girl" (440). Thus, the photograph of Kathleen for James is "Lifelike. Like her" (79). Friendless, Kathleen never quite exists as a human being in her family or her community. From the beginning, in fact, Kathleen was unreal to Materia, "the princess and the pea" (67), and for James "could do no wrong" as "he loves her too much" (35). Materia is unable to love Kathleen and instead sees her as the focus of James' demon: "Materia has two real daughters [Mercedes and Frances] now, she loves them, so it's all very clear" (67). As a result, Materia makes a bargain with the devil: "if the demon will limit itself to one daughter, Materia will allow it to have Kathleen when the time comes" (69). Of course the time does come when Kathleen, the "abandoned mine" (136), dies violently giving birth to her father's children.

In many ways Frances is a parallel to her sister Kathleen. Both experience sexual abuse from their father; both give birth to a child unknown to them; both are involved in an interracial relationship; both are theatrical: Kathleen the would-be "diva" of "legend" (123) and Frances the "great actress" (403); and both are involved in a rape. In fact, Kathleen in her journal has a wild side which she only begins to explore once she wants to be seen as a real person: "I look at myself just to remind myself that I'm there [...] I want someone to see me and touch me before I am old" (459). Unfortunately, Kathleen has only a brief time to step out of the "fading photograph" (459) before she is locked back into its frame. She remains the appropriated photographic object, the *memento mori*, and "a token of absence" (Sontag 16) until she is finally released by Frances through the agency of Kathleen's daughter Lily.

Frances, in contrast, is a montage, "a moving picture" (3). Literally "baptised at the Empire Theatre" (64), she finds the movie theatre her refuge and the films shown there her religion. The Empire, with its "frenetic dance of light and shadow" (46), is the source of Frances' connection with her mother Materia, who, for a time, joyed in playing musical accompaniment on the theatre's piano. This world became her refuge: "she was happy as long as she could play" (53), the place where she found freedom of expression and playfulness in scoring the films and vaudeville performances with "discordant music":

> Now and then a locomotive sped towards the audience through "I Love You Truly," and ran over them to "Moonlight Sonata." Villains struggled with virgins to "The Wedding March" and saved the day to "Turkey in the Straw." Performers complained but the audience ate it up when rabbits emerged from top hats to discordant splats and women were sawn in half to "Nearer My God to Thee" (55).

When James learns of Materia's success, however, and Kathleen's musical gift is associated with Materia ("Gets it from her mother, no doubt"), he passes judgement on "his illiterate wife" and "a low type of music" (53), forcing her to quit her job. Hence the Empire Theatre is a place of resistance and rebellion that, for Materia, unfortunately "receded and became unreal" (55). Quite naturally and inevitably its "ecstatic darkness" becomes Frances' world where she retreats and plays hooky from school.

The film world is where Frances finds her models and standards of behaviour and also her language and expression of values. It is where she first realises her rebellion, her view of men, and eventually her sexuality. Frances not only learns all the lines of the scripts of favorite films but also shocks and scandalises with her intuitive recognition of film erotics. In her comment on Douglas Fairbanks in *The Thief of Baghdad* ("Okay watch, here comes the part where he gets flogged 'n he escapes from the palace and you can see his pecker right through his pants" 197) Frances reveals insight into an unconventional, unspoken, dark erotic world.

Unlike her sister Mercedes and her friends, Frances "has different idols" (197) and sees the behaviour of her favourite film stars not at a distance as the others do but as a direct standard for her own values and behaviour. While Lilian Gish is her model because "She is so small and brave. She can be bent but never broken" Frances arrives at her understanding of men: "Men are brutes and if they are not, they are big galoots or else chivalrous princes who arrive too late" (197). To get money for the movies, she takes from Lily's stash but convinces herself of the justice of this action by using the film world and its language as her point of reference: "Frances only takes what she needs – 'a mere bagatelle'[3] – and she knows Lilian Gish would do the same" (198). Frances even writes to Lilian Gish, but hers is far from the conventional fan letter. The experience of film has resulted in her taking up her own assumed identity or role: a brave, wheelchair-ridden Kathleen Piper with a nice, caring father to look after her. Clearly, Frances writes the letter to Gish from this perspective to achieve a sympathetic response; however, it also expresses an element of poignant wish-fulfilment in the adopting of the identity of the loved daughter.

As Frances matures, she moves from the model of Lilian Gish who is "perfect" (197) to emulating Louise Brooks. While her movie experiences have helped her to expand her imaginings of her family's secrets, this identification with Brooks enacts sexualization and rebellion. Thus, when Frances at sixteen shows up at the speakeasy, she sees herself as "the only fallen princess to have crossed the threshold." In her effort to effect a transformation ("where to begin?"), she envisions a fairy godmother who would "swathe her in ostrich feathers: in breasts, hips, lips and lipstick – a husky contralto which she imagines to be Louise Brooks's voice" (287). Frances consequently goes to the barber shop with "a picture of Louise Brooks" (288) to get her hair cut in the "raven helmet" bob made famous by the actress. Indeed, Frances' decision to go to a barber shop is part of her rebellion. When the barber tells her that he "doesn't know how to cut ladies' hair," Frances announces "I'm not a lady."

Brooks, in temperament and career, is a suitable and informing model for Frances; known as "Brooksie," she was in iconoclast, rebel, and model of the flapper/modern woman. Child of an unconventional family and a mother who had little time for parenting in her outgoing social life, Brooks was already a professional dancer at the age of fifteen; in fact, she had appeared in Canada with Martha Graham's

---

[3] Interestingly, the phrase "mere bagatelle" comes from Louise Brooks' *Diary of a Lost Girl* and not a Lilian Gish film – perhaps an intentional anticipation of Frances' transference of model from Gish to Brooks.

troupe. After making twenty-one silent films in the US, she walked away from her contract, something unheard of, especially among female film stars. Journeying to Germany, Brooks became the focus of the "fetishistic gaze" (Witte 1990: 167) of G. W. Pabst, most noticeably in two of Frances' favourites, *Diary of a Lost Girl* and *Pandora's Box*.

Pabst's two films, which are specifically referenced in *Fall on Your Knees*, present the two complementary sides of the "innocent bad" girl: the innocent girl who looks bad and the bad girl who appears innocent. Frances, by sexually abusing the boy "Puss-Eye" in her school, ensures her expulsion and puts herself beyond James' beatings: "She is as beat as she'll ever be" (291). She has now moved beyond "any lingering faith on anyone's part that deep down Frances was good." James, in fact, associates Frances' new "Brooksie" image with her being beyond his power to shape and control:

> The insolent face, the freshly hacked curls. Lost. And gone forever. What happened to her? My little Frances. James sighs. He can't think about all that right now. There's too much of it. It's too dark in there, and he doesn't have the energy (291).

Frances is now in the "ecstatic darkness" of her movie-generated, inspired life. In fact, dark places like the speakeasy, under her grandfather Mahmoud's bed, the grille behind which she watches Mahmoud' maid Teresa prepare food, and the mine where she seduces Ginger, become the locus and expression of Frances' identity.

In *The Diary of a Lost Girl*, a film which projects "the entire bourgeois world as a function of an inherent sadomasochism" (Schlüpmann 1990: 83), Brooks plays Thymiane, a young innocent exploited by an evil seducer who impregnates her. Once the mother of an illegitimate child, she is cast out by her weak father and conventional middle-class family, finding herself in a cruel reform school where she and the other girls are treated sadistically. Escaping into a life of prostitution, she finds the Berlin brothel at first a place of sexual freedom and female agency, but it eventually becomes the site of "father-daughter reunion" where middle-class exploitation and repressed "incestuous male desire" (Rifkind 42) surface. At a nightclub, where Thymiane raffles herself off to help a man with his finances, she comes face to face with her father. Pabst employs prolonged emphasis on the eye, on father and daughter watching one another; however, because the father is too weak, he abandons his daughter to the exploitation of other men. Eventually, a dignified and elderly Count rescues Thymiane and restores her to a version of the respectable life she had lost. He embodies the noble, salvific side of the father: the one who cares for and loves his daughter enough to take action in spite of the pressures of any conventionality.

A number of elements in *The Diary of a Lost Girl* parallel Frances' life as the daughter "expelled" and abandoned by her father. In fact, "Part 5" of *Fall on Your Knees*, wherein Frances enters the speakeasy world, is actually entitled "Diary of a Lost Girl." By stowing away in James' vehicle as he delivers bootleg alcohol, Frances finds out about the speakeasy: a clear parallel to the Berlin brothel in Pabst's film. The hypocrisy of the weak father in the film is a parallel with James' hypocrisy – passing moral judgement on the speakeasy life while covertly associated with its economy. While Frances is attending the matinee of *The Diary of a Lost Girl*, Ginger follows her, "waits until his eyes resolve the shadows into shapes" (349), and, when the lights go on, "watches" her. The film world effectively seals the attraction Ginger feels toward Frances while the film's concluding moral statement – "IF THERE WERE MORE LOVE IN THIS WORLD, NO ONE WOULD EVER BE LOST" (349) – becomes a most appropriate gloss on Frances' life and the parallels between Thymiane's pregnancy and Frances'.

Frances uses the model of "childishness and androgynous coquettishness" (Schlüpmann 90) in Thymiane's character as her way to "assert her presence in male society" in order to achieve her own ends. In presenting herself as a vulnerable victim to Ginger, she accommodates male narcissistic fantasy. Unlike the world of Pabst's film, however, where woman acts "as a function of masochistic narcissism" (Schlüpmann 88), Frances is fully aware of being in control of this role as is evident in her ironic self-presentation to Ginger, her act of seduction:

"Little Ginger Man… I need someone to look after me. I'm full-grown, but I'm just a little girl inside. I want you to find me 'cause I'm lost, I'm lost in a deep dark place, please, please, please, oh you smell nice'" (336). By presenting herself as small, lost, abused – in need of saving –, Frances arouses Ginger's erotic self: "'Don't leave me please, I'm so frightened of the dark,' closer. 'I won't leave you, but…' he's embarrassed to find out he's hard, he didn't know he wanted her, still doesn't know" (372).

Frances' seduction of Ginger in the mine shows how she can manipulate the "deep dark place" for her own ends. Frances achieves female subjectivity, therefore, by reversing the rape-seduction and exploitation of Thymiane, using the movie image of abandonment to co-opt male power and thus complete "one piece of unfinished business" (336). Ginger, like the Count in Pabst's film, is "the only good man I know." By seducing him, the black man, Frances is able to transgress the incest taboo in an act paralleling James' rape of Kathleen.

Kathleen violates James' vision of her when he discovers her in sexual embrace with her black lover Rose (interestingly, Frances has used the letters R-O-S-E as markers to show the way to mine shaft where she has lured Ginger). By her act of agency and autonomy, Frances uses the framework of Pabst's film and what she has modelled from it to cross the final barrier to her father James. Thus, Frances has effectively restored a balance through her action. Her pregnancy leads to James' confession of his rape of Kathleen, the freeing of Lily, and (although unknown to Frances) the rescuing and reconfiguring of family when her son Anthony goes in search of Lily. *The Diary of a Lost Girl*'s depiction of family as a cruel and unforgiving institution, a "structure" of "particular harshness" (Schlüpmann 81) is familiar ground for Frances. However, the film's "erotic tension" and its "attempt to sentimentalise a prostitute" (Schlüpmann 81) provide Frances with a means to redeemed her life by moving "beyond the social limits that define female sexuality" as she "begins to mine men's bodies for her own gain" (Rifkind 42).

Ginger sees visiting the speakeasy and, thus by extension, contact with Frances the "whore clown," as "entering Pandora's box" (350). The title of Pabst's other film that dramatically sculpts Frances' self-image is, in fact, *Pandora's Box*, and the life and character of Lulu (Brooks) again impacts Frances' views of love and sexuality: "Frances's reflections on the subject of romance are summed up in the last scene of *Pandora's Box*: when Louise Brooks finally gives it away to a fella for free, he ups and kills her" (294). Lulu, a prostitute in Pabst's film, uses her innocent look and her sexuality to seduce and control others, in some cases leading to their death or, at least, their destruction. Schon, a wealthy magnate; Alwa, his son; Geschwitz, a female costume artist – all fall under the spell of Lulu, revealed so effectively throughout the film by gaze, spectacle, and the emphasis on the eye as "organ of desire" (Doane 1990: 67). Schon, who sees his passion for Lulu as his "execution," dies at her feet after struggling with a gun, in his dying breath warning his son to "watch out for that girl." At her trial, Lulu is accused by the prosecutor of opening Pandora's box; however, her innocent eyes effect her escape as the witnessing throng stages a false fire and conceal her, whisking her out of the courtroom. Because her "eyes are generally flirtatious in an indiscriminate manner," many fall under her spell and she achieves control over them. Lulu, as the primary object of the gaze, is thus "the focus of the constant demands and desires of the other characters" (Doane 66).

However, Lulu recognises for a moment the other side of what happens when one becomes "pure image" (Doane 67): "Everyone wants my blood, my life." Inevitably, while in London, she falls under the spell of Jack the Ripper's "small unsteady eyes":

> In his scene with Lulu, as long as the directness of the gaze is sustained (during the eye-line matches between Jack and Lulu) he is docile, almost infantile. His gaze becomes less steady as Lulu leans on his shoulder and closes her eyes. In her moment of repose in the film, she becomes the victim of male psychosis. The eye is not only the organ of male desire, but that of performance and deception as well (Doane 67).

From her own experience with modelling herself on Brooks in the films and witnessing the complex of female sexuality, Frances is equally determined to be militantly in control of her own future:

> She has no intention of leaving the island until she has made enough money for Lily. And accomplished something else too. What, Frances? Something. She will know it when she sees it. She is a commando in training for a mission so secret that even she doesn't know what it is. But she is ready. Every night the obstacle course. Manoeuvring behind the lines. Camouflaged to blend with the terrain (307).

Like Lulu, Frances is able to effect seduction and control and is thus impregnated by Ginger. Also, like Lulu, Frances knows that everyone wants her "blood," her "life." Thus, while she is able to rescue Lily from the family, save her father James though his confession, and even save her sister Mercedes from a life without her and from the lie of Lily's origins, she cannot really save herself. Even her life in her son is taken from her. However, her strongly maintained point of view which the "guardian angel" narrator shares with us and which we embrace gives Frances an extended, enduring life. It's interesting that Brooks was called "Lulu" for many years after filming *Pandora's Box* – and Frances remains the "silent moving" picture well after our reading is done.

V

Toward the conclusion of *The Way the Crow Flies*, the central character Madeleine "has a vision" of the murder of a childhood friend, a memory long lost which surfaces "without her conscious help." MacDonald's emphasis on image, expressed in the words "see," "visual," "illustration," leads to a significant revelation, to the "pour[ing] out of what is within." This revelation invokes for Madeleine what is "behind her eyes": "It fills the screen in Panavision. Shot from below in rich early 1960's pastels, lusher than life, like an illustration from an outdated grade-school reader. Except that this is not a still photo or a drawing" (2003: 696). Madeleine's vision is expressed in the language of film and the tense and syntax of montage with the use of parataxis and present tense verbs: "She smells tar and resin and looks up at the telephone pole." This revelation leads to her exposing what is "still there"; in fact, she realises that "the truth was always there" (697) waiting for the subject to uncover it, waiting to be seen.

MacDonald locates the cinematic, the reel that will run without "conscious help," at the centre of her narratives for both her characters and her readers. For *Fall on Your Knees*, where the style, structure, and thematics are expressed in terms of photography and film, image technologies provide the nexus between object and eye as well as between the eye and the "something else": the psychic depths behind the eye. Such an approach, as Walter Benjamin reveals, "does not simply render precisely what in any case was visible, though unclear; it reveals entirely new structural formations of the subject" (690). As the truth is neither out there nor in here, but only in the dialogue between seer and seen, the "grammar" and "ethics" of film and photography become more than trope or stylistic device for MacDonald. Visual culture is the foundation of our way of seeing and point of view is its expression. This is not a fuzzy, relativistic vision, but acknowledgement of the eidetic, ineffaceable truth which was always there.

CHAPTER 6

Old Texts, New Readings: *The Ledger*, *Steveston* and Picture Poetics

Simona BERTACCO

University of Milan, Italy

> *I can be shamelessly narrative and I find myself the more so as I go on.*
>
> – Robert Kroetsch

> *Language is leafing out, is everything that is growing, that is organisms, that is body. It's a body. I love that phrase, the body of language. And I'm trying to realize its full sensory nature as much as possible.*
>
> – Daphne Marlatt

I. Our Daily Image Intake

In the past decade, some of the works that Robert Kroetsch published in the early 1970s have been republished in editions that have recuperated the original accompanying visual images. This occurrence signals an interesting change of perception of the importance of those images for a full appreciation of Kroetsch's poems and their meaning. I have in mind here especially the twin works *The Ledger* and *Seed Catalogue*, published in book format in 1975 and in 1977, which have been re-issued, respectively, in 1997 by Brick Books and in 2004 by Red Deer Press.

A slightly different destiny has awaited Daphne Marlatt's work of the same period. In the early 1970s, Marlatt was working on an Oral History project for the Provincial Archives of British Columbia concerning the Japanese fishermen town of Steveston, BC, which gave rise to two books: *Steveston* (1974) and *Steveston Recollected* (1975). Both works marked a strict collaboration of the poet with the photographer and artist Robert Minden, but most of the literary criticism devoted to them has consistently focused on Marlatt's poetry alone, relegating the visual element of the books to at best an illustrative and secondary status. *Steveston* has been reissued twice: in 1984 and in 2001 with interesting changes concerning the interplay of poem and photographs.

It is quite obvious that attitudes towards the presence of photographs or drawings in verbal narratives are subject to taste and, as a consequence, to change. Following the history of these works from the early 1970s to the early 2000s will enable us to question the way in which the visual has encroached upon – if it actually has – the literary canon. That our society has by now entered the "Image Age" is, as a matter of fact, a crude platitude. But, if we think about it, we could easily divide up our day and daily activities on the basis of our image intake: dinner in front of the news, weekly appointments with the hottest TV serial, or else with a movie, either at the cinema or at home with a DVD, not to mention the often intrusive advertisements that "escort" us on our way to work, to school, to the shops. Curiously, however, despite their ubiquitous and ever-increasing presence, the status of advertisements in the hierarchy of discourse types is still among the lowest. Ads – whether they be broadcast on TV or printed on billboards, newspaper pages, etc. – are commonly associated with "oral texts," in that they share not only the low esteem in which orality is held by the educated establishment, but also and mostly, the ephemerality of their performance-based existence. Now, it may well be that this dislike of the creativity hidden behind advertisements in our society is due to "a puritanical objection to the idolization of material objects and possessions, and a degree of snobbery about 'trade'" (Cook 1996: 224), as Guy Cook argues, but it seems to me that it is becoming more and more difficult – not to say disputable – to deny on such grounds the craftsmanship implied in many advertising texts circulating today.

What is at stake here is, clearly, the different social statuses of poet and advertiser: the poet's *art* is by definition disinterested, not available on command and, more often than not, hardly a lucrative activity. On the contrary, the advertiser's *craft* belongs to a different category altogether, one that, being dependent on a market-based economy, is automatically mundane and denied entry into the superior sphere in which true art lives.

The figures I have chosen, the poet and the advertiser, are positioned at the extreme ends of the social spectrum and there are indeed many more flexible positions in-between. However, I am convinced that the idea of poetry – rather than of literature *tout court* – is still viewed by most people as superior by reason of its "uselessness" in everyday life and commerce. It is a fact that many Canadian writers – like Margaret Atwood, Robert Kroetsch, Dionne Brand, just to name a few – who started their careers as poets, later turned to fiction in order to make a living with writing. In Canada, moreover, poetry books are almost exclusively published through the federal funding provided by the Canada Council. This picture confirms the general impression that poetry is more "superfluous" than novels and non-fiction books and therefore occupies a much smaller niche in the publishing market.

Speaking of the main features of today's poetic taste, Marjorie Perloff points out that:

> In a contemporary context of one-liners on the TV screen and the computer monitor, as well as lineated ads, greeting-cards, and catalogue entries, the reader/viewer has become quite accustomed to reading "in lines." Indeed, surfing the Internet is largely a scanning process in which the line is rapidly replacing the paragraph as the unit to be accessed (Perloff 1998: 90).

Out of this actual familiarity with printed linearity, one might expect a more active study of the forms of contemporary poetry exactly within the current "context of one-liners" mentioned by Perloff. Today's emphasis on visual modes of communication and artistic representation could provide, therefore, an ideal context for re-reading some of the experimental work produced in Canada in the previous decades, but most of all for "reading" the texts of the present in a way that does not take for granted the hegemony of word over image.

II. Unusual Textualities

If the line can be perceived as the basic unit of poetry in the age of free verse (Perloff 1998: 98), the work of the poets I am going to consider in this essay must be located within a different background: that of Canadian poetics caught between three different impulses: concretism in the 1960s, deconstruction in the 1970s and postmodernism in the 1980s. Robert Kroetsch's *The Ledger* and Daphne Marlatt's *Steveston* were published for the first time in the early 1970s, and still had a vital bond with the great revolution that concrete poetry represented for English-Canadian poetry. Even though neither Kroetsch nor Marlatt ever followed the kind of experimentation embodied in the work of bp nichol, they share with concrete poets a peculiar approach to the poem's graphic surface. Indeed if there is one aspect of the concrete period that has permanently marked Canadian poetry, this surely is the poem layout which has never been quite the same afterwards. In her study of the "new" poetics in Canada and Quebec, Caroline Bayard notes that the "awareness of space as a graphic and signifying agent was to become a permanent addition. [...] Even writers who had never or seldom experimented with concrete techniques had by 1980 abandoned regular margins and straight-lined verse" (Bayard 1989: 163).

The visual legacy of the 1960s does not seem to have been highly appreciated in the following decades, at least as far as the scholarly study of Canadian poetry is concerned. Even though poststructuralism and postmodernism opened up a number of aesthetic possibilities for English-Canadian literature, such as, for instance, an open concept of the text being written and read, and a deep reflection on writing techniques, there seems to have been a resistance – after the heyday of the "visual Sixties" (Bayard 103) was over – to go back to a more traditional (in the sense of language-based) approach to the poetic text.

The reason for this can be found in a widespread "resistance to visual culture generally" (Garrett-Petts & Lawrence 2000: 1) in the academic field which explains why, even among contemporary theorists, there is a tendency to "elide modal differences or otherwise domesticate the visual by regarding it as just one more form of language, as 'text'" (*ibid.* 35). This is the crucial problem that literary readings of hybrid texts have to face and it has something to do with the general distrust of images I mentioned in the introduction: how do we read a text when textuality ceases being an exclusively linguistic product? What enrichment comes into our literary appreciation of a poem from a consideration of its visual illustrations? Does the visual have an impact on how we respond to the text? These are a few of the questions that I will try to answer in my belated reading of the texts by Robert Kroetsch and Daphne Marlatt.

In their ground-breaking work dedicated to the multi-modalities of contemporary Canadian art, Garett-Petts and Lawrence offer a tempting hypothesis: they invoke a "new visual/verbal vernacular" for Canadian literature in which visual, verbal and oral modes converge (6). The innovative element of their reading is that the oral vernacular is shown to find its textual expression in the visual inscription of the text rather than in merely linguistic terms. In other words, what would normally be lost on the printed page – i.e. the accent, the local cadence as reminders of a grounded or real experience – is recuperated and integrated through the visual idiosyncrasies of the text. What is needed, therefore, is what they define as a new "rhetoric of reading," a new concept of textuality, which subsumes the act of viewing as part of the act of reading.

As already mentioned, the reason why I selected Robert Kroetsch and Daphne Marlatt and their works for this paper is the specific time frame and the theoretical environment – deconstruction, postmodernism, feminism – in which they operated. As far as the works that Kroetsch and Marlatt wrote at the beginning of the 1970s, in fact, the deconstructive pull characterizing them was made evident, on the page itself, by the visual apparatus they used. Therefore, it seems remarkable that so little has been said and written about the graphic elements of their works in the past 30 years.

II. Robert Kroetsch & the Poem of the Ledger

In Caroline Bayard's words, the "post-modern imagination rejects linearity. [...] Intersections, palimpsests, and blanks would be more appropriate descriptive tools" (155). Indeed, palimpsests and intersections make up the method of composition of Kroetsch's *The Ledger*, a long poem that keeps the promise borne by its title: in this book, an old financial ledger physically constitutes the palimpsest upon which the text is written. Like its partner poem *Seed Catalogue*, it presents us with the metamorphosis of an object coming from the author's own past. It is a collector's work in that we encounter, in the geo-graphical space of book, charming and spell-casting objects linked to the private reminiscences or personal obsessions of the writer.

The Ledger has led an interesting double life as a book: its first edition as a single book, published by Applegarth Follies, presented a hand-set layout reproducing an old ledger and an old map on which the poem was actually printed, while its later reproductions within Kroetsch's *Field Notes* (1981) and *Collected Field Notes* (1989a) was deprived of its original layout. This reduced the impact of the poem in that it took away from the book as object the physical presence of the "found material," the archaeological frame against which the poem was originally written and read. In 1997, however, *The Ledger* was republished as a volume, most of its original features back in place. I have highlighted five major anomalies distinguishing the "new" ledger from the "old" one:

1. The author's handwritten inscription on the cover-map, reading "Yes. That's the place, RK," and leading to a circle on the map around the village of Kieffer – which actually attracted the eye in the Applegarth Follies' edition – is absent.

2. The two pages of the old ledger belonging to Henry Hauck that are present in the new edition are reproductions of different pages or of different sections of the same ledger, therefore there is not a perfect identity between the two editions.

3. The variety of typefaces used in the original book as well as the "typewritten look" of the page have been replaced – by necessity I imagine – by only one typeface and a regular "printed" outlook.

4. An 1800 map of Upper Canada has been added to mark the end of the book which was not present in the original.

5. In terms of the poem layout on the page, the 1997-edition pages being slightly smaller than the 1975-edition ones, the first lines of the poem have been put at the end of an almost blank page and separated from the first entry of the ledger book which has been pushed at the beginning of the following page. A similar operation has been done at the end of the book, so that the two final lines of the long poem:

REST IN PEACE

You Must Marry the Terror

are placed at the top of an empty page, followed by a blank page reproducing at the very bottom a hard-to-decipher signature.

The type of paper used for this edition (acid-free Zephyr with an antique laid) serves to enhance the quality of old document as well as the grey cover-page with an old-fashioned inscription of the title. This works very well with the general intention, which seems to be the motive behind the very form of the "new" ledger: responding to the continuous demand for a republication of the 1975 *Ledger*, and "selling" the poem as an experimental work, that invites the reader to "shuck the term" of poetry and to "read [her]self in" (back-cover).

So all in all, the work that has been done on *The Ledger* was borne by the idea that *The Ledger* still is "a foundational" poem of Canadian poetry, and that its mixed-media textuality needed to be restored. As a matter of fact, it is a book that presents itself as a book, and a very physical one, as Kroetsch himself recalls:

> I don't know when I began my continuing poem. It was years ago that my Aunt Mary O'Connor, one afternoon at her house in Edmonton, handed me the ledger that had been kept by her father, my grandfather, at a watermill in Bruce County, Ontario. Up until then I'd had no idea that my grandfather and Aunt Mary and I were in complicity. I finished the poem, the poem of the ledger, and called it *The Ledger* (Ondaatje 1979: 311).

The original ledger was "a record of debits, credits, and all money transactions" bought by Henry Hauck, Canadian-born son of a Bruce County pioneer, to hold his sawmill accounts. Robert Kroetsch, his grandson, reads in it "the green poem," and weaves it into another book – the one that we are presently reading. The title page, in the Applegarth Follies' edition, is enclosed between two pages reproducing sections of Henry Hauck's ledger, and it displays a map of the townships of Culross and Carrick, in Bruce County, Ontario, dated 1880. On the map, the note "saw m" is encircled by a thick black line, and a red-ink scrawl reads "Yes, that's the place, RK." From there, the poem unfolds: the old ledger keeping track of family history becomes both an account of a moment in national history and the private imaginative projection of the poet himself. The poem marks the border between History and personal Story and shows their interconnection. More than that, through the geographical grounding of the poem in the land, the poet asserts locality as the guiding principle of his reading of the past and of the present.

Formally, *The Ledger* presents short and repetitive lines. The repetition of the same sentence at the beginning of each line creates an enchanting effect which is enhanced by the layout of the poem and its typographical insistence on certain words. It is the layout – the graphical emphasis given to certain words, the general pattern composed by the words, the lines and the numbers on the page, together with the general columned frame of the ledger – which literally guides our reading. In this sense, *The Ledger* makes up a very physical museum of words, a place where the readers are called, like the visitors of an art gallery, to react empathically and to "make sense" of the scattered collection they are looking at. From the start, then, our eyes are struck by the unusual formal structure of the work: the double column of the financial ledger is reproduced all along and heterogeneous elements are inserted according to a technique that recalls that of the *collage*. Beside excerpts from Henry Hauck's ledger, there are maps, fragments from a historical atlas, census records, letters, newspaper articles, and tombstone inscriptions. As Manina Jones points out, the *collage* technique dislocates the found materials from their original setting, and organises them into a new "ensemble" where they find themselves linked to one another through unpredictable sometimes even forced poetic associations (Jones 1993: 53). The poem, in fact, is striking for its preposterous collisions, especially because its documentary parts retain the flavour of their extra-literary existence. The link with the extra-literary dimension of the "book of the ledger" itself opens up new discursive possibilities, new ways to tell the stories of the place. The graphic aspect of the book, then, is the physical embodiment of the new way of telling stories that Kroetsch is exploring.

The poem as a whole receives its structure from the six dictionary entries of the word "ledger" around which clusters of images and reflections are organised. As the first dictionary entry suggests, the poet's question is how his writing can survive like the old ledger that has outlived its owner:

the	the ledger survived
ledger	
	because it was neither
itself	human nor useful

Through the list of dictionary entries, the ledger as historical document becomes a symbol of how language and culture change, and a parallelism is established between the search for one's language and the search for one's authentic self (Thomas 1980: 17). It is a search proceeding through progressive moments of affirmation and negation, that seem to advance hand in hand, a search that finds in the balancing structure of the ledger its visual icon:

(I'll be damned. It balances.)

yes: no

no: yes

The poem visually confounds content and container and the impossibility of finding a balanced account of oneself is displayed by the double column layout. Poetry and world get fused in the body and in the shape of the poem as the "I" becomes alive as a self-conscious entity only through the telling of its tale. In this light, the ledger is a scaffolding structure whose function is to contain language and to record and organise actual experience. It is language that records history (dates, place-names, people, events). But, as a form of discourse (i.e. a use of language bearing a social function), the ledger has also a history of its own which is inscribed in the forms that it has progressively taken in time. Indeed, it is the recovery of the language of the past contained in the original ledger that offers the poet the starting point for his poetic search (Bertacco 2002: 94-5):

CÈNSUS, I86I: COUNTY OF BRUCE:

2,663 horses	turnips: 848,40 bushels
6,274 working oxen	wheat: 642,110 bushels
19,830 cattle of all ages	maple sugar: 170,365
29,412 sheep and swine	cheese: 24,324 lbs

In the voyage to the past that *The Ledger* describes, language emerges as the instrument as well as object of the poet's quest. The issue of the metamorphic nature of language becomes central from the opening lines and is stressed throughout the poem by the use of dictionary entries, newspaper articles, German inscriptions, or simply by spelling problems:

Henry.	How do you spell maple?	m—a—b—l—e
Henry.	How do you spell balance?	b—a—l—l—o—n—s
Henry.	How do you spell Henry?	H—e—n—e—r—y

But the ledger is not simply found material, it is also *inherited.* Indeed, this ensures that a personal and communal link to the outside world enters its narrative and protects it from attacks of unbridled textuality. A letter by "Aunt Mary" the one who gave Kroetsch the ledger is inserted in the corpus of the poem and carries the idea of a family legacy:

Dear Bob,

... In regards to information about my Grandmother – your great Grandmother – Theresia Tschiart. She was a sedate tall heavyset person, well read and could visit with the best. She did love reading and mixing with people. She was widowed three times before going west... She passed away after trying to sit on a chair and missing it, broke her hip and was in bed for a few weeks, died and was buried in Spring Lake, Alberta. She was still very active before her fall ...

all my love
Aunt Mary O'C

Being a record of debits and credits, the poem is characterised by a give-and-take structure, which gives an idea of the interconnection between the present and the past:

my grandfather, Henry (dead)
in his watermill (gone)
on Teeswater River,
on the road between Formosa and
Belmore, needing a new ledger:

the ledger itself (surviving)
purchased in the Bruce County
Drug and Book Store (Price:
$ 1.00 PAID), the leather cover
brown. In gold: THE LEDGER:
EVERYTHING I WRITE
I SAID IS A SEARCH
(is debit, is credit)

As E. D. Blodgett (1984) has noted, the page here becomes a picture-space in which the horizontal and vertical movements of the clusters of lines alternate with each other and in some sections, like the one above, the reading can proceed in both directions. As a consequence, meanings are multiple as the six dictionary definitions of the word ledger, each unlocking a different vision of the past, exemplify. But more than that, in my opinion, what the reading of this poem records is a movement from vertical to horizontal reading, or a mixture between the two in which no one knows if there actually is a right way of doing it. This is explicitly stated in the "picture-poem" of the first and last editions. This is not say that Kroetsch's postmodern preoccupation with the issue of reading disappears once we take away the maps of the townships of Culross and Carrick, or the pages of his grandfather's ledger, since it is still captured in the scaffolding layout of the poem. However, the sensuous aspect of the pleasure of reading and of leafing through the text with the illusion of turning the pages of an old ledger is quite lost when we read the poem within *Field Notes* and *Collected Field Notes*.

Kroetsch's attempt to expand the expressive potentialities of poetry has led him to explore, in order to find his poetic voice, a new and unconsecrated "grammar" of poetic composition, but he has also devised texts that call for a reading process which slowly and patiently grows familiar with his hybrid texts. Therefore if the vertical reading practice is almost unanimously conceived as the "proper" one for poetic texts, in this long poem Robert Kroetsch is ostensibly disturbing any form of automatic engagement with the text, starting from the hierarchy between the visual and the verbal elements on the page. Almost inadvertently, we are led by hand by the author to start, not from the lines of the poem, but from the scribbled maps and the old documents it has grown out of. We strain our eyes in the effort to recognise a town we know or to decipher – in the Applegarth Follies' edition – the hand-written inscriptions. In the reproduced sections of the old ledger, then, we try to understand the types of objects that were bought, the operations that were recorded, the names or the occupations of the people involved in the transactions, as so on and so forth. Thus, when we finally get to what we may think is the long poem "proper," we are not totally surprised at finding even more lists of money paid or received, census data, tomb inscriptions, old letters, etc. Only at this point do we realise that we have been reading/viewing the poem since the very beginning and that the "grammar of delay" (Kroetsch 1989a: 117) which made us linger on one or another aspect of the cover page or of the book is going to be the only way in which we can read a poem like this one. The real question about *The Ledger* should be: how are we supposed to read this text? Are we truly invited, as the blurb of the 1997 edition says, to become writers, to add our inscription in the poem, in order to understand it?

If this is the case, as I believe it is, the reader has to be willing to learn to read through the text, to take delight in the documentary minutiae and, most of all, in establishing horizontal associations among the heterogeneous elements encumbering the page. In their book, Garett-Petts and Lawrence have underlined the similarity between the horizontal allegorical principle and cinematic techniques:

> A horizontal orientation calls for a different kind of associative practice, one that has more in common with putting together the frames of a film, the

images in a dream, or the hyperlinks in the World Wide Web (Garrett-Petts & Lawrence 2000: 62).

There is a construction process underlined in the poem as the ledger is defined:

b. "a horizontal piece of timber, secured to the uprights supporting the putlogs in a scaffolding, or the like."

However, the construction work that is in progress leaves the montage a rough cut in that it deliberately juxtaposes as incompatible elements the scattered marks left by lived experience. As a matter of fact, even though relations and connections are important in this long poem, separation remains and, actually, the grandfather's text is always kept in one column separated from his grandson's by a white space running between the two. No real fusion, no visual connection takes place.

The use of sketches and fragments that we saw enacted in *The Ledger* provides Kroetsch with the possibilities of a new narrative dispensation, one that employs cuts, flashbacks, montage and particular layout. The book is like an exploration site and, like all explorations, it requires patience and carefulness. *The Ledger* is a work that literally "pays back" the patient reader, not so much in terms of a final pattern or unity to be drawn out of it, but rather in terms of the intense pleasure that results from reading it.

III. Daphne Marlatt & the Poem of the River

"It is difficult to read Daphne Marlatt's poetry without *seeing* the river" (Lecker 1978: 56) [my emphasis]: these words open Robert Lecker's critical appreciation of Marlatt's poetic production up to *Steveston,* but in fact they capture perfectly the intense sensory experience that Marlatt's poetry offers to the reader. Marlatt's deep interest in the local seems to have derived – initially – from her strong desire, as an adolescent, to feel part of the country in which she had moved with her family from Malaysia, but most of all from her poetic beginnings in the wake of Black Mountain and TISH poetry:

> Olson taught me the importance of roots in a locale, which is probably, apart from the fact that I love the city, why I went back to Vancouver. It's a geography I grew up with and I'm still fascinated by it. And then too – so far I've been talking about sources, but something even more basic than that – Creeley, Olson, Duncan all talked a lot about language, its roots, the way it moves. I mean that is so basic that I can't even think of it in terms of "influence": simply, they opened up the whole activity of writing for me (Marlatt 1977: 29).

Marlatt's writing has been open from the beginning to the transcription of her bodily perceptions, of her present condition of writer in the act of writing. In her poetry the printed word, like a seed, is physical, it has a body and is repeatable and generative. Her interest in etymology and in the various languages of a culture (what Bakhtin defined *heteroglossia*) leads her to listen carefully to the voices of the people surrounding her and to interweave all the voices into the texture of her work. Hers is a complex poetry, a poetry that asks its readers to make their way through its labyrinthine structures.

In *Steveston*, published for the first time in 1974 and republished twice – respectively, in 1984 by Longspoon Press, and in 2001 by Ronsdale Press – the writing process captured in the book encounters place and time in the memories of the people from Steveston. The original idea came to Marlatt in the early Seventies when she was working on an Oral History project for the Provincial Archives of British Columbia about the Japanese fishermen town, the result of which was published in 1975 under the title *Steveston Recollected. Steveston* marks a collaboration of the poet with the photographer Robert Minden. In this work, which critics still view as among her best achievements, the poet allows Steveston in its totality (the river, the town, the people, the work, the memories, the disillusion, etc.) to get to her and pass through her, and the poem becomes a cosmology in its ability of "eat[ing] up the whole world" (Miki 1989: 40).

Whereas in my reading of Rober Kroetsch's poem – where the first edition is essential to grasp fully the reason behind the "restoration" work done to the most recent edition of *The Ledger* – I moved back in time (from the 1997 ledger to the 1975 one), in this part of the essay I would like to move forward in time, focusing my analysis on the most recent edition of *Steveston* (2001) as an instance of a successful postmodern experiment with the documentary genre still viable today.

seeking to perceive it as it stands…

JAMES AGEE

This is the book's epigraph, recalling another inter-artistic collaboration: the one between the poet James Agee and the photographer Walker Evans in the mid-1930s entitled *Let Us Now Praise Famous Men*. In this way, the book calls forth the conscience out of which it has originated and, in a subtle way, it also establishes its readership (Garrett-Petts & Lawrence 2000: 262): those people who are acquainted with, and appreciative of, such hybrid art forms. In the following page, we see the first photograph by Robert Minden, framing, in the foreground, a white wooden house resting on pilings on the river, gill nets at the front, a curtained window through which the back of a white fan is visible; in the background, a spot of untidy vegetation set against the grey sky, two dark wooden huts, and, occupying the lower third of the picture, the river itself. This is the visual introduction to the latest edition of *Steveston*. The major difference between the three editions consists in the more inclusive design of the later ones. If in the first edition of *Steveston*, Minden's photographs occupied the first half of the book and Marlatt's poems the second, in the 1984 and 2001 editions, the two narratives are interwoven together according to the artists' changed perception. As Marlatt explains in "Distance and Identity: A Postscript to *Steveston*":

> In 1984 we have gained some distance on that book and see its story as a single narrative told in two distinct modes that wind around each other. [...] Ten years ago we wanted to highlight the difference, the distance between our two "takes," although we had been working very collaboratively for over a year and despite the fact that both photography (as its name asserts) and poetry are forms of writing, one with light, the other with words (Marlatt 1984b: 42).

Fixity and flux are the vital elements around which there grows, just like the "green poem" that Kroetsch wrote on his grandfather's ledger, Marlatt's poem of the river. In her works, fixity often identifies the land and the sense of stability it irradiates, while flux refers to the changing ability that time brings to the land itself. The meeting at the crux of space and time gives reason to the quality of instantaneous perception of the immanent world pervading Marlatt's lines. The sense of being there and the moment of poetic creation coincide, so that the one cannot exist without the other:

> The focus is not so much on looking back as on moving towards something the poem will put together. It seems to have to do with the construction of something against nothing, against the emptiness that underlies it all. (Marlatt qtd. in McGuirk 1994: 77).

In one of the early critical essays on Marlatt, Rober Lecker underlines how her poems are always seeking "the precision, objectivity, and instantaneous image implied by the photograph," so it comes as no surprise that "her books are progressively characterised by an application of photographic principles" (Lecker 1978: 65). In Lecker's terms, "*Steveston* is composed of a photographic poetry of immanence" (*Ibid.*) which finds in the actual photographs by Robert Minden its counterpart.

That the visual is tantamount to Marlatt's writing is indeed clear since the opening of the first poem of the book, "Imagine: a town." The pause, symbolised by the column, between the imperative verb and the object is pregnant with the expectation of a *tableau* taking shape in front of our eyes. The poem interlocks with Minden's photograph of the previous page on two levels: there (in the photograph) we could see three wooden houses on the river; here (in the poem) we imagine what happened to those wooden houses during the fire which struck Steveston in 1918. There we saw three seemingly isolated huts on a river; here we start glimpsing at what is going on inside those little houses. The words of the poem fill the thick white space framing all the photographs in the book: so neatly do the pictures stand out on the whiteness of the page, so widespread on the page are the poem's lines. On page 14, we actually read the lines that turn into words the first image of Steveston the book offers:

> But she is in her
>
> element, dreaming of sails, her father's, of a friend's son, at the
>
> Imperial which owns their boat, their net, their debt. But the
>
> Frazer gives of itself, incessantly, rich (so the dream goes),
>
> & wooden houses jammed on pilings jammed together, leaning, with
>
> wooden walks & muddy alleys, laundry, & the dry marsh grass that
>
> stutters out of silt the dykes retain, from a flowing
>
> ever eroding & running river… (Marlatt & Minden 2001: 14).

In her "Postscript to Steveston," Daphne Marlatt wrote that "Robert was drawn primarily to people, to specific people, who, like messengers, announced themselves to his camera." Instead she "was drawn to the river, to the tidal flow at the Fraser's mouth where it pours into the sea, as much as to the people who had spent most of their lives in this place" (Marlatt 1984b: 43). When reading the book as a whole, Marlatt's words seem to irradiate from the photographs, not only because she writes down the language of the place which is heavily linked to what the people living there have told her, but also because she writes down, in words, the process of coming to terms, entering the new place, and getting involved in it and by its people. In the same postscript, Marlatt writes extensively about the sense of being outsiders – linguistically, culturally and professionally – that she and Minden shared and of the creative impulse this generated: "There was something in Steveston which drew us, over and over again, and which our work attempted to enunciate" (*Ibid.* 42). In the opening movements, the poem is unmistakably identified with the river: it is the poem of the river. When, eventually, the people of Steveston are described, they take on the aspect of marine or submarine creatures. The adjectives qualifying them are in fact taken from the vocabulary of river and sea that Marlatt is exploring, therefore when the salmon industry has finally passed under the control of a multinational company, it is the people's lives that are packed up for good, the same way as they are packed up in the "Orchard," the internment camps in New Denver where many Japanese Canadians were sent after Japan's attack on Pearl Harbor in 1941: "a residue of pain, dug into the land" (Marlatt & Minden 2001: 39).

There is an interesting occurrence of a clear separation of the poet's voice from that of the people whose lives she is weaving into her own net. The sharp tone of the following exchange between the poet and two fishermen:

> Are you going to raise that pole? I'd like to watch.
>
> She wants to watch! (Laughing, he says something in Japanese to the other two.) You gonna *help*? (27)

triggers the acknowledgement of the difference between the voice of the poet and the voice of the people. Textually, it marks quite a unique moment in the book, where the dialogue sections occur sparsely, and must have been seen as an act of honesty by Daphne Marlatt herself. The overall impression, in fact, is that the statements of the people met or interviewed are conveyed by the photographs in which they stare right into the viewer's eyes, whereas Marlatt's poem builds up the web of relations between the river, its people, and Steveston.

Two movements seem to dominate the imagery of both poems and photographs: the village, its workers, and their legacy are sinking down ("this town down stream its own downpour..." 16), the sign that the times when the canning industry was flourishing are long gone. A "curious backwater/stillness" hovers over the town, turning its boats into ghost vessels where unaware children can play and make up stories of adventures and "secret catch[es]" (26). On the contrary, amid the wasteland images that keep recurring along the poem, the "corporate growth" of Vancouver's suburbia is relentless and pervasive, as well as its horizontal extension, changing as it proceeds the outlook of the town, transforming the winding path of Moncton street into a straight line ("a line that lies" 31); and drying out, with the closing down of the cannery industry, the lives of all the men and women who used to live by the river: fishermen, cannery workers, children.

In the last poem of the first and second edition, the whole story of "Steveston, B. C." is finally rehearsed by the chiming repetition of the name of the town followed by four different descriptions of its reality:

> Steveston: delta, mouth of the Fraser where the river empties, sandbank after sandbank, into a muddy Gulf.
>
> Steveston: onetime cannery boomtown: "salmon capital of the world": fortunes made & lost on the homing instinct of salmon.

Steveston: home to 2,000 Japanese, "slaves of the company": stript of all their belongings, sent to camps in the interior away from the sea, wartime, who gradually drift back in the '40's, few who even buy back their old homes, at inflated prices, now owning modern ranchstyle etc, & their wives working the cannery, have seniority now, located.

Steveston: hometown still for some, a story: of belonging (or is it continuing? lost, over & over… (56).

The use of a colon to separate the name of the town and its subsequent descriptions gestures back to the first poem of the book and its invitation to "Imagine: a town": *this* is the town, and these are only four of its real and possible images. The poem is turning towards its close. There is a sense of final balance being done, of nostalgia for "the people, whose/history locates inside of dream" (57). Following a series of sequences in which the dominant image was that of rotting corpses and "decomposed ground choked by refuse, profit & the concrete of private property" (52), there comes Marlatt's latest version of Steveston, the poem she wrote for the 2001 edition, entitled "generation, generations at the mouth."

Searching for "the body's blueprint" (61), the poem drifts up source, imitating the salmon in its return towards the river source to die. The mouth of the river has now turned into "a toxic O of emptiness," the "teeming hole of/ever-becoming we create" (62). A final metamorphosis, however, is on its way:

> at the mouth of the river, clans of the possible are gathering, the chinook,
>
> the coho rivering just offshore are us (62).

The conversion of noun into verb (*rivering*) marks the final movement of the long poem: it is we who have "lost the verb in our/currency" (62), possibly, by letting Steveston rot in the water, but we too stand for the past, since we are excluded by the clans of the possible that are gathering, now, at the mouth of the river.

In their analysis of Marlatt and Minden's work, Garrett-Petts and Lawrence identify in the book a "collision (or collusion) of modernist and postmodernist aesthetics" (Garrett-Petts & Lawrence 2000: 268), where the modernist component is attributable to the formalism of Minden's photographs, the postmodern one to the process of Marlatt's poem in the act of being written. What they see as an opposition between Minden's "modernist aesthetics" and Marlatt's "river of words" (*Ibid.* 265) could be, in my opinion, resolved in a more flexible image if we took into consideration at least one of Marlatt's works in which the graphic and visual elements come in as complementary integrations of the verbal. The work I have in mind is *How Hug a Stone* (1983), a long poem in the form of a travelogue in which a highway map is reproduced, on a different scale, in various sections of the book. Ostensibly, the function of the map – on which the author's hand has circled the places already visited and added the missing names of the tiny villages she has passed through – is to allow the reader to follow the persona's trip, therefore progressing also the horizontal and narrative trajectory of the story. More subtly, however, the "tampered" map – as both written text and re-written by the author – serves to ground the book deep in a specific place or locale, therefore implying that locality is the actual place where writing occurs. The search for the language in place and of place in language are the generative principles of Marlatt's writing (Bertacco 1998: 146), leading her to resort to the help of non-verbal modes of communication: visual (the maps, inscribed and signed by the narrator) and aural (achieved mainly through puns and word games with Old English words).

Read in the light of Marlatt's writing of the same years (*How Hug a Stone* was published in 1983) *Steveston* – particularly in its 1984 and 2001 versions – in its entirety appeals to me as an attempt to overcome any rigid demarcation between the typologies of its graphic inscriptions: with light or with words (Marlatt 1984b: 42). A very visual poet since her earliest works, Marlatt has continued to include the visual in her own flux of words, perceptions and sensations. As she says: "I want the process to always be *visible*, the feeling of the state evoked" (Marlatt 1989: 25) [my emphasis], and she uses whatever means she has at her disposal to convey, in the immanence of the book, all the layers of her intellectual, physical and emotional experience of writing.

IV. Conclusion: Page-Specific Poems

Both Robert Kroetsch and Daphne Marlatt share an interest in local history and their excavations of ordinary and of vernacular language – especially in Kroetsch's case – have literally mapped the textual territory of Canadian postmodern poetics. As a matter of fact, Kroetsch's and Marlatt's poems, although they look and sound very different (Kroetsch's lines are little black marks on the white page, whereas Marlatt's extend, like a net, from margin to margin), are page-specific, in that they take the page as frame, and within this frame they deploy their materials – be they words, images, photographs, maps – in a way that requires not only a writing process open to external craftsmanship, but also a reading sensibility prepared to take in all the aspects of their textualities.

The texts by Kroetsch and Marlatt that I have looked at in this essay, by virtue of the intriguing editorial lives they have led, were and still are experimental for the way they flow between the documentary privileging of the tokens of experience – which the use of photographs, author-modified maps, palimpsests provides – and the vernacular voice or storytelling which is implied in the narrative potential of the long poem. What seems to emerge from the reading of the latest editions of *The Ledger* and *Steveston* is that the "particulars of place" (Kroetsch 1989a: 76), in very different ways for each poet, suggest a powerful formula for dislocating the written word from the page. Their use of the visual element enables them to achieve a new animation of the text: place names, newspaper headings, old photographs, business ledgers, diaries, journals, tall tales come alive as possible points of entrance into the poetry of place. The central concept for both writers – and the reason for which I decided to bring their works together – is the link to the place their poetries grow out of and the "alphabet of place [that they write] in more ways than one" (Kamboureli 1991: 123).

Concluding with the questions I set out to tackle in my essay, could we interpret these poems without relating their words to the images or the photographs they contain? I hope I have shown how much of the poems' pregnancy is actually lost if we only read, without seeing, these poems.

CHAPTER 7

Dialectical Images in Canada: Joseph Dandurand, Stan Douglas & The Conjectural Order

Richard J. LANE

Vancouver Island University, BC, Canada

Kwantlen First Nations poet and playwright Joseph Dandurand and photographer/film installation artist Stan Douglas both utilise dialectical images of Canada as a medium for cultural and artistic exploration, producing in the process internationally known works. The term "dialectical image" derives in this usage from the work of Walter Benjamin, where dialectics at a standstill is the actuality or "now of knowability" brought about by the interruption of historical contemplation with the collocation of recently outmoded objects and ideas that reveal concrete (and potentially revolutionary) insights concerning the present. As I argue elsewhere: "Benjamin's historical materialism is not an attempt to uncover the constructedness of history, its fictional status as theorised by postmodernists, but is instead a destruction of the 'fictions' of a commodified or hyperreal world, an unleashing of forces which occur simultaneously with 'the birth of authentic historical time'" (Lane 2005: 65). The point of reading Dandurand and Douglas using the concept of the dialectical image is to avoid recycling tired notions of postmodernism and/or image manipulation, and to show how both artists create powerful, revolutionary images that *cross* and at times *disrupt* theoretical domains, or, more accurately speaking, are complex constellations. As Benjamin argues:

> To thinking belongs the movement as well as the arrest of thoughts. Where thinking comes to a standstill in a constellation saturated with tensions – there the dialectical image appears. It is the caesura in the movement of thought. Its position is naturally not an arbitrary one. It is to be found, in a word, where the tension between dialectical opposites is greatest. Hence, the object constructed in the materialist presentation of history is itself the

dialectical image. The latter is identical with the historical object; it justifies its violent expulsion from the continuum of historical process (475).

Both Dandurand and Douglas also engage with the performative in their image production: for Douglas, this involves processes of digital control and random film-looping, for example his installation work *Journey Into Fear*; for Dandurand the performative is theatre, for example with his two "cigar store wooden Indians" who are the protagonists of his play *Please Do Not Touch The Indians*, or, the images that are juxtaposed with his poems in his book *looking into the eyes of my forgotten dreams*, which will be of concern here. In many ways seemingly different artists, I am bringing Dandurand and Douglas together to create my own montage or creative-critical constellation, which links with postcolonial counter-discourse (Cf. Lane 2006a: 27), but also to think about how indigenous and other Canadian peoples are represented and recoded in their work. With Douglas the main images I will focus on are his photograph called *Every Building On 100 West Hastings* and the images that make up his multi-media text *Journey into Fear*; with Dandurand the main photograph studied is found twice in his poetry collection *looking into the eyes of my forgotten dreams*, but I will focus on its use in conjunction with, or as part of, his poem "Fort Langley"; the photograph is by Frederick Dally, and it is titled "Indians, Fraser River circa 1868."

My theoretical argument, in summary, is that:

- both Douglas and Dandurand create what Walter Benjamin calls "dialectical images"
- in both instances, regardless of the variations in technologies used, the images are created via montage
- in both cases the dialectical images create a powerful "memorial aesthetics" which is both a memorialisation and an intervention in the present-day representation of indigenous and other peoples in Canada.

Dandurand & *Fort Langley*

Fort Langley

you can see the fort from where I live.

wooden walls,

trees,

desperate voices.

they call to me,
come on over,
come on over,
come on.

shut up,
I say.
shut up and stay over there.

used to drink at their bar,
used to sip whiskey,
used to fight,
used to be blind from it all.

now
I stare at their walls.
wooden walls.
thick with history.

many men and women never made it home.
they found them trying to climb over the walls.
whiskey bottles broken and empty roll down to the
river,
laceless shoes sit silent as if waiting for someone else,
a picture of someone's mother blows away and over the
walls,
the gate is closed.

the fort.
over that way.
over past the mass grave.
smallpox.
you ever seen smallpox?
pretty ugly.
not as pretty
as wooden walls (6-7).

The poem is not printed in isolation: it works in conjunction with a powerful image, one of the many that Dandurand found while browsing in his local library at Fort Langley, BC, one of the images which he wanted to reclaim.[1] The image is cropped, which is understandable, given the caption handwritten by Dally directly onto the photograph: "Indians shamming to be at prayer for the sake of photography. At the priests request all the Indians kneel down and assume an attitude of devotion. Amen" (Davison 1981-82: 19). The word "shamming" juxtaposed with the image-based photographic performance is intriguing; also, the spurious homonymic etymology that could produce a link with "shaman." Dandurand has recoded the "sham" here: instead of indigenous peoples performing a mode of belief that was imposed upon them by colonialism, the image is now seen as a "sham" imposed by Dally, i.e., he becomes a *synecdoche* and repetition or return of that colonial imposition. Instead of indigenous peoples looking foolish here, Dandurand creates a pathos in his juxtaposition of photograph and poetic text, which recodes the actors in the photograph in a subversive manner. This recoding is not simply a postcolonial reversal; instead, it creates a dialectical image, a "now of recognizability" whereby images are subtracted from "sham" narratives of progression or evolution, and exposed instead to a different configuration which has an explosive potential. Why explosive? Because dialectical images simultaneously function as memorial aesthetics and a rupture in time. For example, after a huge amount of work has been done by critics cataloguing, critiquing, and rejecting "inauthentic" images of indigenous peoples, e.g., the work of Curtis, indigenous peoples in the US and Canada are re-appropriating those very same images and giving them a new value, inserted into a new context, with *recoded memorial significance*. This is a radical gesture of re-recognition and a temporal intervention, although such a process generates what Lyotard calls "a differend": non-indigenous academics want to condemn "sham" colonialist images while respecting at the same time the right of indigenous peoples to assert critical and creative autonomy in their use of them; holding both contradictory positions together is a differend, or, the recognition in law that both sides here have a legitimate claim. From either side of the issue, the differend does not exist; but juxtaposed, as in a montage, the differend

[1] This reading of Dandurand's work is also my identical starting point in an essay called "Sacred Community, Sacred Culture: Authenticity & Modernity in Contemporary Canadian Native Writing," in Deborah Madsen (ed.), *Native Authenticity: Transnational Perspectives on Native American Literary Studies* (SUNY UP, 2009). In this latter paper I develop my reading in relation to Dandurand's *Please Do Not Touch The Indians*.

does exist, with powerful repercussions. We can of course think about this issue in the context of treaty negotiations.

Douglas and *Every Building On 100 West Hastings*

Every Building On 100 West Hastings appears to be a wide-angle photograph of the 100 block in Vancouver's downtown eastside. The inhabitants of this neighbourhood are often homeless or low-income people, drug users and sex-trade workers. Many indigenous peoples, especially vulnerable young women, have been abused and murdered in this neighbourhood over the last few decades, a haunting fact considering that Douglas's image is devoid of human beings; another reason for this absence is that the 100 block is part of a neighbourhood that property developers are planning to demolish and rebuild, with high-end loft apartments, condos and office space. What has this got to do with Dandurand's recoding of text and image? First of all, Douglas's image is a deliberate "sham" in the postmodern sense of being digitally manufactured: it isn't a wide-angle lens image at all, and it presents a picture that no single point-of-view could reproduce:

> Douglas shot twenty-one photographs, which loosely correspond to the number of lots on the block, on the night of August 27-28, 2001 [...] and converted them into digital imagery with a high resolution scanner. The artist meticulously sutured these representations together on a computer using microscopic digital pixels to blend the joins between the individual shots and smooth out their perspectival disjunctures. He then printed the image in two parts using a light jet printer, seaming them together at the centre to form a sixteen-foot panoramic vista of the entire block (Oleksijczuk 2002: 108).

The word "panoramic" gives us a clue as to the status of this image: while it utilises many of the technologies of virtual reality and postmodern hyperreality, it also utilises a slightly older technology, that of the montage, even if the end result is a montage without borders. In other words, the suturing together of scanned images means that the original images were not in digital format and that they have been converted into a hyperreality that still maintains connections with the modernity of second-order simulation. So why is this a dialectical image? I suggest that the resistance to a singular point-of-view and the absence of human beings points to and foregrounds the desired and ongoing evacuation of this urban space which is actually home to many people; the evacuation is coercive: the removal of tenants through various legal or illegal means. There is also an allusion in this absence to the murder of many of the neighbourhood's inhabitants. For example, the Missing Women's Task Force in this area was set up after media and other pressure to investigate missing sex-trade workers and others; the fact that a serial killer was at work in the neighbourhood had not been deemed worthy of initial investigation by the authorities because of the low status – or lack of status – of the killer's victims. So while Douglas's image is ostensibly of a neighbourhood in its "death throes," the image is also a memorialisation through absence of all of those individuals, known and unknown, who have been murdered in their downtown eastside homes. The montage works by intersecting the homely and the unhomely, or the homely and the uncanny: there is absence or death where we expect life, and life where the commercial redevelopers of this neighbourhood want us to perceive absence (or death). This connects with Dandurand's dialectical images in *looking into the eyes of my forgotten dreams*, where the text is "about" the impact of the residential school experience for Kwantlen First Peoples, and also the intersection of the homely and the unhomely or uncanny. The residential school, supposedly a place of care, was of course also a place of abuse; some of those in charge, who had the legal status of guardians or parents, also engaged in a cultural genocide project. I do not wish to reduce the complexities of this historical event, one which I believe is integral to understanding Canada's relationship with its indigenous peoples; I am merely pointing out that the memorial aesthetics of both Dandurand's and Douglas's dialectical images reject mainstream Canadian narratives of humanistic progress, and instead return to certain architectonic sites and imagistic sights for reasons of critical intervention.

As noted, the dialectical image is a key part of what Benjamin calls "dialectics at a standstill" explored most profoundly in his *Arcades Project* and "On The Concept of History"; but why in this case "dialectics" at all? I argue that it is crucial to separate and distinguish such a montage image from a fully commodified and commutable "hyperreal" image of the sort theorised by Jean Baudrillard and others (Cf. Lane 2000). In other words, dialectics at a standstill, while initially theorised by a messianic German-Jew at the time Europe became overshadowed by the horrors of Nazism, is a large enough concept to deal with modern technologies of representation *and* notions of the mysterious and the sacred, such as indigenous belief systems; in other words, Dandurand and Douglas either want, or inadvertently produce, a more radical if not revolutionary notion of the image, one that does not engage in a postmodernist abandonment of the sacred or the *traces* of humanity.

PoMo Vancouver: Permutational Narrative Images

Douglas's *Journey into Fear* is a multiple series of texts, first and foremost being a film installation with a large number of permutations: "a picture track loops while its dialogue tracks are constantly changing" (Douglas 2002b: 26). The setting of the film is a container ship heading into the port of Vancouver, with two main characters visibly on board: Möller and Graham. Möller is a "supercargo," an individual who deals with the passage of sensitive, dangerous or simply extremely valuable goods, while Graham is a ship's pilot. It is the film's form and timeline, however, that is the most obvious complicating device, making strange the normal chronological development of narrative:

> The timeline is broken in four positions (1-4) to permit branching. At these junctures, a computer randomly chooses which one of five dialogue variations (A-E) will be performed. Each time the picture track repeats, a different combination of dialogue segments is heard until all permutations have been presented. There are 625 possible combinations, however, this script [the Serpentine publication] presents only five. Segment 1A is here followed by 2A, although it might very well be followed by 2B, 2C, 2D, or 2E – just as 2A could be followed by 3A, 3B, 3C, 3D or 3E, etc.
>
> Additionally, there are two variations of picture track montage and performance blocking. In one, for example, Möller passes a letter to Graham, and in the other Graham passes a letter to Möller. Between the interior dialogue variations, two halves of a foot chase are presented. One complete loop of the picture track is thus composed of four sections... (Douglas 2002b: 26).

Journey into Fear is also a printed document, composed of: a film script, temporarily "frozen" into five permutations with visuals, essays ("*Journey into Fear*: An Introduction"; "*Journey into Fear* and Melville's *The Confidence-Man*"), the author's comments ("*Journey into Fear* [2001]") and a series of photographs (*Journey into Fear: Pilot's Quarters 1* [2001]; *Journey into Fear: Pilot's Quarters 2* [2001]; *Damaged Continers, Mitchell Island* [2001]; *Every Building on 100 West Hastings* [2001]; *Rookery, Burnaby* [2001]; and *Impounded Fishing Vessels, North Vancouver* [2001]). While the printed document can only give a sampling of the film installation, its own complex arrangement of different written and visual texts/images is mimetic of the installation's complex form and functioning. Intertextual relations are also flagged up, as Matt Thorne notes: "Stan Douglas's film installation has one timeline derived from *Journey into Fear*, a twice-filmed thriller based on an espionage novel by Eric Ambler, and four from *The Confidence Man, His Masquerade*, a novel by Herman Melville" (2002: 19). Intertextuality, while commonly thought of in terms of thematics and the transference of iconic objects and characters, also functions at the level of form. As Thorne suggests:

> Douglas has described his project as a "machine," stating that, "like any machine, this 'remade' *Journey into Fear* has the effect of transforming time into space, by translating mutability and transience into a constellation of elements that are simultaneously present within a defined system." It has been argued that Melville designed *The Confidence-Man* to be a project of endless possibilities (20).

One of the most representative aspects of the text's postmodernism is the fact that it is produced via a constantly morphed environment: that is to say, the location of the installation and/or text is divided internally and externally, so that naturalistic mimesis falters. The claustrophobic setting of the cargo ship means that mimesis is in fact cliché, but not necessarily in a negative sense: it is the cliché or recycling of statements as such from other films, other dramatic performances. The cargo ship is moving towards the port of Vancouver (the plot of the bifurcated sequence is that Möller wants to delay the ship's arrival), but within the parameters of the story world, it never arrives; whereas Malcolm Lowry's *October Ferry to Gabriola* is driven by the desire for arrival, *Journey into Fear* is driven by the necessity to slow down the arrival of the ship. Vancouver is in fact the destination that is never represented, or, represented in its absence. The latter has, in some quarters, become a way of identifying Vancouver's uniqueness: that it can stand in for some place else, which means that "it" disappears as such in the process. Stephen E. Miller calls this notion of identity "cultural schizophrenia" and he argues that it: "has been the norm for so long – almost two decades – that for artists and craftspersons living in the city it has become a point of intense pride that, with a little preparation, Vancouver can become virtually anything, anywhere, anytime" (1994: 283). Implicit in this statement is the notion that Vancouver is more than just a city that becomes a morphed setting; rather, there is the finer point, *that Vancouver itself is the work of art*, the plastic substance that can be moulded and shaped in myriad ways. This can be seen in the work of Jeff Wall, which can be read as an *interpretation* of Vancouver as a specific locale. As Trevor Boddy notes, after seeing Wall's work at an exhibition at the Institute of Contemporary Arts in London:

> it was quite evident that specific conjunctions of landscape, capital, and passions in these suburban Lower Mainland [of Vancouver] venues could not be substituted for other locales; they literally could not be 'replaced.' His [Wall's] readings of place were specific and resonant, even if the sites of their consumption as images were elsewhere (1994: 45).

Even though Vancouver is the absent referent of *Journey into Fear*, failing to be placed directly (in itself, a complex notion) in representational space, *this is still a way of representing Vancouver's specificity*; indeed, one of the main intertexts of *Journey into Fear*, the 1975 motion picture with the same name, was itself filmed in Vancouver. The sequential *re-makes* thus perform the same acts of erasure and aporetic *affirmation* of setting.

The text of *Journey into Fear* does juxtapose the aporetic installation extract with the sorts of photographed locations expected of, say, Vancouver photographer Jeff Wall; the similarities may not be entirely accidental, for example, Douglas's photograph of *Impounded Fishing Vessels, North Vancouver* (2001) not only has the vast blue Vancouver sky as the background, with the industrial vessels and dock lamps in the foreground, but there is also a compressed and flattened view of downtown Vancouver, all of which is reminiscent of Wall's *The Thinker* (1986). In fact, Douglas's *Impounded Fishing Vessels, North Vancouver* is in many respects the reverse image of Wall's *The Thinker*; the latter print has downtown and the north shore as the background, and is taken from the land mass we are looking at as the background of *Impounded Fishing Vessels, North Vancouver*. In both shots the image is cut horizontally by a line, which creates a right-angle with a lamp-post: in Wall's image the horizontal line is a power or phone line, in Douglas's it is a cloud trail possibly caused by an aeroplane. In both shots, downtown Vancouver is framed, and sits behind, industrial landscapes; in both shots the space is divided into three blocks. Perhaps the only significant difference between the two shots (apart from the fact that they are almost mirror images structurally and formally speaking) is that Wall has a human subject posed dramatically on the right-hand side of the image, while Douglas has focused on the absence of human subjects, represented by the three bicycles parked at the base of a ramp leading up on to one of the ships. As such, these photographs function very differently, although they are both very carefully composed and framed. An even more significant photograph that accompanies *Journey into Fear* is *Every Building on 100 West Hastings*; Borchardt-Hume, for example, argues that this photograph firmly locates the overall setting of the film installation (2002: 17). Looking closely at this photograph, as noted above – the viewer notices no people whatsoever, and more significantly, the subject matter is a series of shop buildings that are semi-derelict or run-down, and/or up for sale. The relationship between the film installation and the photograph *Every Building on 100 West Hastings* is clearly one which focuses on their oppositions: the installation is a self-enclosed space generated via postmodern intertextuality whereas *Every Building on 100 West Hastings* is mimetic, being *literally* a photograph of an entire block of buildings. The latter are not represented, however, in the modernist sense of achievement and dominance of the urban space, rather, the evocation of impending doom or redevelopment is closer to the driving force of perpetual exile found in Malcolm Lowry's Pacific Northwest writings, particularly *October Ferry to Gabriola*. Rebuilding is a postmodern process par excellence: it signifies not the possibility that the city space can be transformed, but that it must *always* be in the process of transformation. The latter, taken to its logical conclusion, means that buildings themselves represent their own destruction and transformation, at all times. This may simply be processed as spatio-temporal confusion, or, architectural complication; as Fredric Jameson suggests, with the Bonaventure Hotel in mind, postmodern buildings

> no longer attempt, as did the master-works and monuments of high modernism, to insert a different, distinct, an elevated, a new utopian language into the tawdry and commercial sign-system of the surrounding city, but on the contrary, seek to speak that very language, using its lexicon and syntax, that has been emblematically 'learned from Las Vegas' (1998: 11).

The apparent signification of potential destruction and rebuilding generated by *Every Building on 100 West Hastings* is not utopian, rather, it is one of semiotic replication and morphing within the lexicon which Jameson is elaborating upon. Baudrillard asks if postmodern architecture has gone beyond what has conventionally been accepted as the "architectural":

> Is this still architecture, this pure illusionism, this mere box of spatio-temporal tricks? Ludic and hallucinogenic, is this post-modern architecture?
>
> No interior/exterior interface. The glass facades merely reflect the environment, sending back its own image. This makes them much more formidable than any wall of stone. It's just like people who wear dark glasses. Their eyes are hidden and others see only their own reflection. Everywhere the transparency of interfaces ends in internal refraction. Everything pretentiously termed "communication" and "interaction" – walkman, dark glasses, automatic household appliances, hi-tech cars, even the perpetual dialogue with the computer – ends up with each monad retreating into the shade of its own formula, into its self-regulating little corner and its artificial immunity (1988: 59-60).

For Baudrillard, postmodern architecture is a detachment from the city space rather than an expression of its language; in other words, Baudrillard has a conception of the city space that he is holding outside of, possibly before, postmodernism, one which is real, rather than hyperreal. Douglas, in the collection of texts called *Journey into Fear*, appears to have a chiastic notion of representing Vancouver; whether this means that Vancouver can be infinitely and solipsistically morphed, in a private, self-enclosed hyperreality or language game, or, whether this is a reflection upon contemporary reality for this major Pacific Northwest city, remains to be seen.

Images of Architecture: Modern vs. Postmodern

An apt comment made by Douglas in his own reflections on *Journey into Fear* is that the historical placing of his installation is ambiguous: it could be now, or it could be the 1970s, the setting of the original film's re-make. Apart from the fact that this ambiguity doubles the temporal ambiguity of the re-make itself, it could also be taken as an unwitting comment on Vancouver architecture. If *Journey into Fear* speaks the architectural language of postmodern Vancouver, then how do we account for the vast amount of unimaginative, dull and dreary modern architecture in Vancouver? If postmodernism is a recycling of the past, sampling or quoting it as part of a new process of aesthetic construction, then how can some of the most boring architecture in the western world be accommodated in this scheme of things? These questions are mediated by a contemporary novella, Mark Macdonald's *Flat* (2000). Like Douglas's collection of texts, Macdonald's *Flat* is a multimedia production: the novella is composed of hand-drawn maps, architectural drawings, and photographs of Vancouver's West End, as well as the written narrative, each chapter being given a location instead of a more traditional number or subtitle. The opening chapter, "#805 – 1461 Harwood Street" juxtaposes a photograph of a modernist apartment block with the narrative concerning the death of "J" the mysterious object of the protagonist's obsession. J lies sprawled, dead, surrounded by pills and alcohol, but also more interestingly "journals and pads filled with frantic notes, sketches and diagrams" (Macdonald 11). There are more materials pasted onto the wall:

> The walls here are entirely covered. He has collaged a million scraps and postcards, writings, news clippings, paintings, photographs, maps. No one looking for the first time would recognise a pattern, but he knew how to read it all. Drawings of buildings around the West End, with pure, even lines, and from dozens of angles, are stacked neatly beside rows of sagging book cases. Above the couch, above the body, there is a large satellite image of the whole neighbourhood, stolen with care from the city archives (Macdonald 11-2).

The novel switches to the first person in the second chapter, "#318 – 1235 Nelson Street," and the story-line connects with this unnamed narrator, a distant friend of J's, who has been contacted to deal with the J's "estate." Death as an inconvenience – see Jim Crace's *Being Dead*

(Lane 2003) – shifts to becoming a drawn-out post-mortem that impacts upon the living. The unnamed narrator, in cleaning through J's flat, discovers that the collage on the wall actually has a depth to it, it is a palimpsest made up of layers: "pictures behind pictures, layers of images and words sometimes four deep" (Macdonald 21). As with Beckett's *Trilogy* and Paul Auster's *The New York Trilogy*, the unnamed narrator eventually appears to morph into J, for example, becoming addicted to the Flutoxocet drug that he has overdosed on. What sends the unnamed narrator "crazy" is his attempt to make sense of the collage and the notebooks that he has discovered. The novella also has a self-reflexive, mirroring quality that both frames and exceeds J and the unnamed narrator; there is the resident of "2401 Comox" in chapter three who lives next door to the resident of "2402," both of these characters reflecting upon one another; there is yuppie who takes over J's flat at "805 Harwood" with no idea that a man has died in it; and the voyeurs at "1005 Harwood" who have watched J's life and death, the new yuppie moving in and the unnamed narrator go insane. Finally, the novella switches to the perspective of the landlord of the unnamed narrator's flat, who is already mentally planning the eviction of this man who has deteriorated so suddenly. Creating analogies with the right-angle in Douglas's and Wall's photographs, this self-reflexive mirroring suggests a non-organic equivalent to the industrial landscapes of Vancouver: in this case, the brutalist architecture of the residential West End, which reached some kind of apotheosis, ironically, with the campus of Simon Fraser University in Burnaby, BC, which Paul Delaney has called "the most imposing monument of late modernism in Canada" (16).

Dialectical Image Morphs Into The Conjectural Order

Dandurand's montages create permutational looping between printed and photographic texts; this permutational looping is also apparent in Douglas's suturing of images-without-end and experiments in film narrative. I suggest that such permutational looping creates a dialectics at a standstill, where recoding intensifies the image so much that it becomes "explosive" and reaches a point of what Benjamin calls "profane illumination." This intensification, also partakes of what I have called the Conjectural Order (Lane 2006b). The Conjectural Order is a re-staging of subjectivity, "one which occurs in everyday life when a crisis point has been reached or a transformational event occurs"; it is also a powerful psychoanalytical investment and projection of "the auto/biographical subject" (Lane 2006b: 80). The dialectical image, thought via the theory of the Conjectural Order, can also be theorised "as a desublimatory convergence of fluctuating intensities or tonalities"

(Lane 2006b: 84), the discourse drawing here upon the work of Deleuze, Guattari, and Klossowski. What I am suggesting, in conclusion, is that Dandurand and Douglas work with transcultural dialectical images, that cross theoretical and national domains, images that cannot be reduced to traditional representational or more contemporary postmodern and postcolonial categories. Both artists under consideration produce explosive images that deconstruct *and* reconstruct notions of subjectivity and place, therefore the return to Benjamin's ideas in this context is productive in the sense of the radical metaphysics at work in the images under study, where "that which seems wholly esoteric and impenetrable" in the montage form, "becomes lucid and full of meaning" (Buse *et al.*, 105). The postmodern draining away of "meaning" is of course re-charged in the intensities produced by various critical and artistic assemblages; in the Conjectural Order, the re-staging or re-performance of subjectivity bridges the deconstruction of the subject and the previous metaphysical reliance on the subject. The bridging is not intended as a synthesis or unification, but more an awareness of the importance of new subjectivities in Canadian First Nations writing, and, in the artistic outputs from the ever-morphing, but still Canadian, ethnically diverse city of Vancouver.

Notes on the Contributors

Simona Bertacco

Dr. Simona Bertacco is Assistant Professor of English literature at the University of Milan. Her areas of specialisation are Canadian literature in English, postcolonial studies and translation studies. Her publications include: *Out of Place: The Writings of Robert Kroetsch* (2001), *Postcolonial to Multicultural: An Anthology of Texts from the English-Speaking World* (2004), *Sul corpo: Culture/Politiche/Estetiche*, co-edited with Nicoletta Vallorani, Cisalpino (2007), and "Postcolonialism" in *The Oxford Handbook for Philosophy and Literature*, OUP (2009).

Lucia Boldrini

Dr. Lucia Boldrini teaches English and Comparative Literature at Goldsmiths University of London. Her publications include *Joyce, Dante, and the Poetics of Literary Relations* and *Biografie fittizie di personaggi storici*, as well as an edited volume on *Medieval Joyce*. She has co-edited a volume of essays on *Autobiografictions* for the journal *Comparative Critical Studies*, and is currently co-editing one on *Folly*. She has published a number of articles on modernist medievalism, comparative literature, fictional autobiography, and literature and science. Her new book on fictional autobiography should be completed in 2009. She is the General Coordinator of the European Network of Comparative Literary Studies, and is a member of the British Comparative Literature Association.

Ron Bonham

Dr. Ron Bonham recently retired from Vancouver Island University, Canada, where he taught Film and Literature, and Film Studies courses. He studied film at The University of Manitoba, and co-directed the Malaspina Film Series, Vancouver Island, for over thirty years. He has presented academic papers on film and literature at the annual Film and Literature conference in West Virginia. His main interests are film adaptation and adaptation theory, as well as the incorporation of film techniques into fiction.

Carmen Concilio

Dr. Carmen Concilio teaches Literatures in English at the Faculty of Modern Literatures and Languages of the University of Turin, Italy. She has published on Nino Ricci, *Roots and Frontiers* (Turin, 2003), on Salman Rushdie, in E. Linguanti, V. Tchernichova (eds.), *The Great Work of Making Real. Salman Rushdie's "The Ground Beneath Her Feet"* (Pisa, 2003), and on Anita Desai, in M. K. Bhatnagar, M. Rajeshwar (eds.), *The Novels of Anita Desai* (New Delhi, 2000), she has co-edited the volume *Coterminous Worlds. Magical Realism and contemporary post-colonial literature in English* (Amsterdam, 1999). She has published several essays on postcolonial literature and mainly on Canadian, Australian and South African writers, such as Ondaatje, White, Malouf, Coetzee and Gordimer. Her most recent publication is C. Concilio (ed.), Ivan Vladislavic, *Johannesburg. Street Addresses*, Tirrenia Stampatori, Torino, 2007.

Keith Harrison

Dr. Keith Harrison lives on Hornby Island, BC; he teaches creative writing, Shakespeare, and film in the English department at Vancouver Island University, Canada. He has written half a dozen well regarded books of fiction, including *Eyemouth* (1990), *Furry Creek* (1999), and *Elliot & Me* (2006); he also edited *Islands West: Stories from the Coast* (2001). Harrison has published widely on Canadian literature, with emphasis on Malcolm Lowry, which was the topic of his doctoral dissertation at McGill University. His current non-fiction project retraces familial links between Tokyo, Melbourne, Prague, Vancouver, and St Ives.

Richard J. Lane

Dr. Richard J. Lane teaches in the English department at Vancouver Island University, BC, Canada, where he is the Director of the Literary Theory Research Group and Seminar for Advanced Studies in the Humanities. He is the author or editor of eight books, including most recently *Reading Walter Benjamin: Writing Through The Catastrophe* (2005), *The Postcolonial Novel* (2006) and *Fifty Key Literary Theorists* (2006); Lane's *Jean Baudrillard* (Routledge, 2000), has been translated into Japanese and Korean, and is available in an expanded and revised second edition (2009). Lane writes the "Canada" section of *The Year's Work in English Studies*, for The English Association and Oxford University Press, and he is currently writing *A History of Canadian Literature* for Routledge. He has published widely on Canadian literature, postcolonial literature and literary theory.

Jeffrey Orr

Dr. Jeffrey Orr is Assistant Professor of English at Beykent University, Istanbul, Turkey. He received his doctorate from The University of Leeds (2006) and specializes in the relations between written and visual texts such as photographs and maps. He is currently researching Canadian and comparative literature, as well as contemporary poetry and small press publishing. He is also working on a book about photography in the work of Michael Ondaatje, W. G. Sebald, and Orhan Pamuk.

Frances Sprout

Dr. Frances Sprout teaches in the English department at Vancouver Island University, Canada. The topic of her doctoral dissertation was the trope of the family photograph and its role in Canadian elegiac family romances. Among her research interests are subjectivity and/in the family; the photograph (especially fictional ekphrasis of same); mourning and memorialisation; visuality within narratives; and, more recently, West Coast and British Columbian literature.

References

Agee, James and Walker, Evans. 1980. *Let Us Now Praise Famous Men*. 1939. Boston: Houghton-Mifflin.

Atwood, Margaret. 1972. *Survival: A Thematic Guide to Canadian Literature*. Toronto: Anansi.

Bakhtin, Mikhail. 1981. *The Dialogic Imagination: Four Essays*. Michael Holquist (ed.). Trans. Caryl Emerson and Michael Holquist. Austin: University of Texas Press.

Banting, Pamela. 1995. *Body, Inc*. Winnipeg: Turnstone Press.

Barbour, Douglas. 1993. *Michael Ondaatje*. New York: Twayne.

Barthes, Roland. 2000. *Camera Lucida: Reflections on Photography*. Trans. Richard Howard. London: Vintage.

Batchen, Geoffrey. 1997. *Burning with Desire: The Conception of Photography*. Cambridge, Mass.: MIT Press.

Baudrillard, Jean. 1994. *Simulacra and Simulation*. Trans. Sheila Faria Glaser. Ann Arbor: University of Michigan.

Baudrillard, Jean. 1988. *America*. Trans. Chris Turner. London & New York: Verso.

Bayard, Caroline. 1989. *The New Poetics in Canada and Quebec: From Concretism to Post-Modernism*. Toronto: University of Toronto Press.

Bazin, André. 1980. "The Ontology of the Photographic Image" in Alan Trachtenberg (ed.) *Classic Essays on Photography*. New Haven: Leete's Island Books, pp. 237-44.

Benjamin, Walter. 1999. *The Arcades Project*. Trans. Howard Eiland and Kevin McLaughlin. Cambridge, Massachusetts & London, England: Belknap Press of Harvard University Press.

Benjamin, Walter. 1992a. "The Task of the Translator" in Hannah Arendt (ed.) *Illuminations*. Trans. Harry Zohn. London: Fontana Press, pp. 70-82.

Benjamin, Walter. 1992b. "Theses on the Philosophy of History" in Hannah Arendt (ed.) *Illuminations*. Trans. Harry Zohn. London: Fontana Press, pp. 245-55.

Benjamin, Walter. 1985. "The Work of Art in the Age of Mechanical Reproduction" in Gerald Mast and Marshall Cohen (eds.) *Film Theory and Criticism: Introductory Readings*. 3rd ed. New York: Oxford University Press, pp. 675-94.

Benjamin, Walter. 1980. "A Short History of Photography" in Alan Trachtenberg (ed.) *Classic Essays on Photography*. New Haven: Leete's Island Books, pp. 199-216.

Benjamin, Walter. 1969. *Illuminations*. Hannah Arendt (ed.). Trans. Harry Zohn. New York: Schocken.

Berry-Flint, Sarah. 2004. "Genre" in Toby Miller and Robert Stam (eds.) *A Companion to Film Theory*. Oxford: Blackwell, pp. 25-44.

Bertacco, Simona. 2002. *Out of Place: The Writings of Robert Kroetsch*. Bern: Peter Lang.

Bertacco, Simona. 1998. "(Re)Writing the Alphabet of Place: A "Nomadic" Reading of Daphne Marlatt's *How Hug a Stone*" in Isabella M. Zoppi (ed.) *Routes of the Roots. Geography and Literature in the English-Speaking Countries*. Rome: Bulzoni, pp. 139-53.

Blodgett, Edward D. 1984. "The Book, Its Discourse and the Lyric: Notes on Robert Kroetsch's *Field Notes*" *Open Letter* 5th ser. 8-9, pp. 195-205.

Boddy, Trevor. 1994. "Plastic Lion's Gate: A Short History of the Post Modern in Vancouver Architecture" in Paul Delany (ed.) *Vancouver: Representing The Postmodern City*. Vancouver: Arsenal Pulp Press, pp. 25-49.

Borchardt-Hume, Achim. 2002. "*Journey into Fear*: An Introduction" in Stan Douglas, *Journey into Fear*. London: Serpentine Gallery & Köln: Verlag der Buchhandlung Walther König, pp. 7-18.

Bowden, Tim. 1985. *Changi Photographer: George Aspinall's Record of Captivity*. Sydney: Australian Broadcasting Corporation.

Bowen, Deborah. 1988. "In Camera: The Developed Photographs of Margaret Laurence and Alice Munro" *Studies in Canadian Literature* 13.1, pp. 20-33.

Brittain, Donald and Owen, Don (dir.), 1965. *Ladies and Gentlemen... Mr. Leonard Cohen*. National Film Board of Canada.

Brossard, Nicole. 1993. "Afterword" in Michael Ondaatje. *Running in the Family*. Toronto: McLelland and Stewart, pp. 179-82.

Brown, Mark H. and Felton W. R. 1955. *The Frontier Years: L. A. Huffman, Photographer of the Plains*. New York: Henry Holt & Co.

Brooks, Louise. 1982. *Lulu in Hollywood*. 1974. Minneapolis: University of Minnesota Press.

Buse, Peter, Ken Hirschkop, Scott McCracken and Bertrand Taithe. 2005. *Benjamin's Arcades: An unGuided Tour*. Manchester & New York: Manchester University Press.

Bush, Catherine. 1994. "Michael Ondaatje: An Interview" *Essays on Canadian Writing. Michael Ondaatje Issue* 53, (Summer), pp. 238-49.

Cadava, Eduardo. 1992. "Words of Light: Theses on the Photography of History" *Diacritics*, 22.3-4, (Fall-Winter), pp. 84-114.

Coetzee, J. M., 1991. *Age of Iron*. New York: Vintage.

Coetzee, J. M., 1977. *In the Heart of the Country*. London: Secker & Warburg.

Cohen, Leonard. 1993. *Stranger Music: Selected Poems and Songs*. Toronto: McClelland & Stewart.

Cohen, Leonard. 1966a. *Beautiful Losers*. Toronto: McClelland & Stewart.

Cohen, Leonard. 1966b. *Parasites of Heaven*. Toronto: McClelland & Stewart.

Cohen, Leonard. 1964. *Flowers for Hitler*. Toronto: McClelland & Stewart.

Cohen, Leonard. 1961. *The Spice-Box of Earth*. Toronto: McClelland and Stewart.

Cohen, Leonard. 1956. *Let Us Compare Mythologies*. Toronto: McClelland & Stewart.

Concilio, Carmen. 2003. "'Worthy of the world': The Narrator/Photographer in Salman Rushdie's *The Ground Beneath Her Feet*" in Elsa Linguanti and Viktoria Tchernichova (eds.) *The Great Work of Making Real. Salman Rushdie's* The Ground Beneath Her Feet. Pisa: ETS, pp. 117-27.

Cook, Guy. 1996. "Language Play in English" in Janet Maybin and Neil Mercer (eds.) *Using English: From Conversation to Canon*. London & New York: Routledge, pp. 198-227.

Cook, Rufus. 1999. "Being and Representation in Michael Ondaatje's *The English Patient*" *Ariel* 30.4, (October), pp. 35-49.

Cooke, John. 1996. *The Influence of Painting on Five Canadian Artists: Alice Munro, Hugh Hood, Timothy Findley, Margaret Atwood, and Michael Ondaatje*. Lewiston, New York & Lampeter: The Edwin Mellen Press.

Corrigan, Timothy and White, Patricia. 2004. *The Film Experience: An Introduction*. New York: Bedford/St. Martins.

Damisch, Hubert. 1980. "Five Notes for a Phenomenology of the Photographic Image" in Alan Trachtenberg (ed.) *Classic Essays on Photography*. New Haven: Leete's Island Books, pp. 287-90.

Dandurand, Joseph A. 2004. *Please Do Not Touch The Indians*. Candler, NC: Renegade Planets Publishing.

Dandurand, Joseph A. 1998. *Looking into the eyes of my forgotten dreams*. Wiarton, Ontario: Kegedonce Press.

Davison, Robert J. 1981-82. "Turning a Blind Eye: The Historian's Use of Photographs" *BC Studies* 52, (Winter), pp. 16-38.

Dawson, Carrie. 2000. "Calling People Names: reading imposture, confession, and testimony in and after Michael Ondaatje's *The English Patient*" *Studies in Canadian Literature* 25.2, pp. 50-73.

Delany, Paul. 1994. "Introduction: Vancouver as a Postmodern City" in Paul Delany (ed.) *Vancouver: Representing The Postmodern City*. Vancouver: Arsenal Pulp Press, pp. 1-24.

Deleuze, Gilles and Guattari, Félix. 1989. *Anti-Oedipus: Capitalism and Schizophrenia*. Trans. Robert Hurley, Mark Seem and Helen R. Lane. Minneapolis: University of Minnesota Press.

Doane, Mary Ann. 1990. "The Erotic Barter: *Pandora's Box* (1929)" in Eric Rentschler (ed.) *The Films of G. W. Pabst: An Extraterritorial Cinema*. New Brunswick: Rutgers University Press, pp. 62-79.

Douglas, Stan. 2002a. *Every Building On 100 West Hastings*. Vancouver: Contemporary Art Gallery/Arsenal Pulp Press.

Douglas, Stan. 2002b. *Journey into Fear*. London: Serpentine Gallery & Köln: Verlag der Buchhandlung Walther König.

Dubois, Philippe. 1995. "Photography *Mise-en-Film*: Autobiographical (Hi)stories and Psychic Apparatuses" in Patrice Petro (ed.) *Fugitive Images: From Photography to Video.* Bloomington & Indianapolis: Indiana University Press, pp. 152-72.

Duffy, Dennis. 1994. "A Wrench in Time: A Sub-Sub-Librarian Looks beneath the Skin of a Lion" *Essays on Canadian Writing* 53, (Summer), pp. 125-40.

Fairley, Ian. 2004. "Doing Translation" *Stand: Translation Special Issue* 5.3 No. 176, pp. 20-1.

Fairley, Ian. 2000. "Parallel Texts" in Olive Classe (ed.) *Encyclopedia of Literary Translation into English.* Vol. 2 M-Z. London: Fitzroy Dearborn Publishers, p. 1040.

Findley, Timothy. 1995. *The Piano Man's Daughter*. Toronto: HarperCollins.

Finkle, Derek. 1994. "From Page to Screen: Michael Ondaatje as Filmmaker" *Essays in Canadian Writing* 53, (Summer), pp. 167-86.

Flinn, Caryl. 1998. "Containing Fire: Performance in *Paris Is Burning*" in Barry Keith Grant and Jeannette Sloniowski (eds.) *Documenting the Documentary: Close Readings of Documentary Film and Video*. Detroit: Wayne State University Press, pp. 429-45.

Frizot, Michel (ed.), 1998. *A New History of Photography*. Bonn: Könemann.

Frizot, Michel. 1998. "1839-1840. Photographic Developments" in Michel Frizot (ed.) *A New History of Photography*. Bonn: Könemann, pp. 23-31.

Frye, Northrop. 1967. *Anatomy of Criticism: Four Essays*. New York: Atheneum.

Garrett-Petts, W. F. and Donald, Lawrence. 2000. *Photographic Encounters: The Edges and Edginess of Reading Prose Pictures and Visual Fictions.* Edmonton: University of Alberta Press.

Ghosh, Amitav. 2007. *Incendiary Circumstances. Chronicle of the Turmoil of Our Time*. New York: Houghton Miffin.

Hallstrom, Lasse (dir.), 2000. *Chocolat*. Miramax, USA.

Handling, Piers. 1985. "Grierson, John" *The Canadian Encyclopedia*, p. 775.

Hart, Josephine. 1996. *Damage*. London: Random House.

Heble, Ajay. 1990. "Michael Ondaatje and the Problem of History" *Clio* 19.2, pp. 97-110.

Hirsch, Marianne. 1997. *Family Frames: Photography, Narrative, and Postmemory*. Cambridge, Mass.: Harvard University Press.

Holbrook, Susan. 1997. "Mauve Arrows and the Erotics of Translation" *Essays on Canadian Writing* 61, (Spring), pp. 232-41.

Hutcheon, Linda and Richmond, Marion (eds.), 1990. *Other Solitudes: Canadian Multicultural Fictions*. Toronto: Oxford University Press.

Hutcheon, Linda. 1988. *The Canadian Postmodern: A Study of Contemporary English-Canadian Fiction*. Toronto: Oxford University Press.

Hutcheon, Linda. 1985. "'*Running in the Family*': The Postmodernist Challenge" in Sam Soleki (ed.) *Spider Blues: Essays on Michael Ondaatje*. Montréal, Canada: Véhicule Press, pp. 300-14.

Jacobs, Johan U. 1997. "Michael Ondaatje's *The English Patient* (1992) and Postcolonial Impatience" JLS/TWL. (June/Junie), pp. 92-111.

Jameson, Fredric. 1998. *The Cultural Turn: Selected Writings on the Postmodern*, 1983-1998. London & New York: Verso.

Jewinski, Ed. 1994. *Michael Ondaatje: Express Yourself Beautifully*. Toronto: ECW Press.

Johnson, M. K. 1993. "(Re)framing the Photograph" *Word & Image* 9.3, (July-Sept.), pp. 229-44.

Jones, Manina. 1993. *"That Art of Difference": Documentary Collage and English-Canadian Writing*. Toronto: University of Toronto Press.

Jones, Manina. 1989. "*The Collected Works of Billy the Kid*: Scripting the Docudrama" *Canadian Literature* 122-3, pp. 26-38.

Kamboureli, Smaro. 1991. *On the Edge of Genre: The Contemporary Canadian Long Poem*. Toronto: University of Toronto Press.

Kamboureli, Smaro. 1988. "Outlawed Narrative: Michael Ondaatje's *The Collected Works of Billy the Kid*" Sagetrieb 7.1, pp. 115-29.

King, Thomas. 1991. *Medicine River*. Toronto: Penguin.

Klossowski, Pierre. 1997. *Nietzsche and the Vicious Circle*. Trans. Daniel W. Smith. Chicago: University of Chicago Press & London: Athlone.

Kogawa, Joy. 1983. *Obasan*. Toronto: Penguin.

Kroetsch, Robert. 2004. *Seed Catalogue*. Winnipeg: Turnstone Press.

Kroetsch, Robert. 2002. "A Conversation with Robert Kroetsch" in Simona Bertacco (ed.) *Out of Place: The Writings of Robert Kroetsch*. Bern: Peter Lang, pp. 221-51.

Kroetsch, Robert. 1997. *The Ledger*. London, Ontario: Brick Books.

Kroetsch, Robert. 1989a. *Completed Field Notes: The Long Poems of Robert Kroetsch*. Toronto: McClelland & Stewart.

Kroetsch, Robert. 1989b. *The Lovely Treachery of Words: Essays Selected and New*. Toronto: Oxford University Press.

Kroetsch, Robert. 1981. *Field Notes: 1-8. A Continuing Poem*: The Collected Poetry of Robert Kroetsch. Don Mills: General.

Kroetsch, Robert. 1977. *Seed Catalogue*. Winnipeg: Turnstone Press.

Kroetsch, Robert. 1975. *The Ledger*. London, Ontario: Applegarth Follies.

Lane, Richard J. 2006a. *The Postcolonial Novel*. Cambridge: Polity.

Lane, Richard J. 2006b. "Theorizing the Gendered Space of Auto/Biographical Performance via Samuel Beckett and Hans Bellmer" in Sherrill Grace and Jerry Wasserman (eds.) *Theatre and AutoBiography: Writing and Performing Lives in Theory and Practice*. Vancouver: Talon, pp. 72-88.

Lane, Richard J. 2005. *Reading Walter Benjamin: Writing Through the Catastrophe*. Manchester & New York: Manchester University Press.

Lane, Richard J., Rod Mengham, and Philip Tew (eds.), 2003. *Contemporary British Fiction*. Cambridge: Polity.

Lane, Richard J. 2003. "The Fiction of Jim Crace" in Richard J. Lane, Rod Mengham and Philip Tew (eds.) *Contemporary British Fiction*. Cambridge: Polity, pp. 27-39.

Lane, Richard J. 2000. *Jean Baudrillard*. London & New York: Routledge.

Lecker, Robert. 1978. "Daphne Marlatt's Poetry" *Canadian Literature* 76, (Spring), pp. 56-67.

Lepage, Mark. 2008. "Cohen Takes Manhattan" *National Post*, Wed., March 12, B3.

Lowry, Glen. 2002. "Between *The English Patients*: Race and the Cultural Politics of Adapting CanLit" *Essays on Canadian Writing* 76, (Spring), pp. 216-46.

Lunson, Lian (dir.), 2005. *Leonard Cohen: I'm Your Man*. USA.

MacDonald, Ann-Marie. "Interview with the Author" Oprah Book Club. 28 June 2005, http://www.oprah.com/obc/pastbooks/annmarie_macdonald/obc_20020405_profile.jhtml.

MacDonald, Ann-Marie. 2003. *The Way the Crow Flies*. Toronto: Alfred A. Knopf Canada.

MacDonald, Ann-Marie. 1996. *Fall on Your Knees*. Toronto: Vintage Canada.

Macdonald, Mark. 2000. *Flat*. Vancouver: Arsenal Pulp Press.

MacLennan, Hugh. 1959. *The Watch that Ends the Night*. Toronto: Macmillan.

MacLulich, T. D. 1981. "Ondaatje's Mechanical Boy: Portrait of the Artist as Photographer" *Mosaic* 14, 2, pp. 107-19.

Marlatt, Daphne and Minden, Robert. 2001. *Steveston*. Vancouver: Ronsdale Press.

Marlatt, Daphne. 1996. *Taken*. Concord, Ontario: Anansi.

Marlatt, Daphne. 1994. "From the Moment Out" Interview by Kevin McGuirk. *Windsor Review* 27.1, pp. 76-84.

Marlatt, Daphne. 1993a. *Ghost Works*. Edmonton: NeWest.

Marlatt, Daphne. 1993b. "When We Change Language…" Interview with Janice Williamson. *Sounding Differences: Conversations with Seventeen Canadian Women Writers*. Toronto: University of Toronto Press, pp. 182-93.

Marlatt, Daphne. 1989. "Correspondences: Selected Letters" *Line* 13, pp. 5-31.

Marlatt, Daphne and Minden, Robert. 1984a. *Steveston*. Vancouver: Talonbooks.

Marlatt, Daphne. 1984b. "Distance and Identity: A Postscript to *Steveston*" *Line*, pp. 42-4.

Marlatt, Daphne. 1983. *How Hug a Stone*. Winnipeg: Turnstone Press.

Marlatt, Daphne. 1977. "There's this and this connexion: An Interview with Daphne Marlatt" *Contemporay Verse* 2 3.1, (Spring), pp. 28-33.

Marlatt, Daphne (ed.), 1975. *Steveston Recollected: A Japanese-Canadian History*. Victoria: Provincial Archives of British Columbia.

Marlatt, Daphne and Minden, Robert. 1974. *Steveston*. Edmonton: Longspoon Press.

Márquez, Gabriel García. 1971. *One Hundred Years of Solitude*. Trans. Gregory Rabassa. New York: Avon.

McDougall, Russell. 1987. "A Portable Kit of Images': Photography in Australian and Canadian Literature in English" *Kunapipi* 9, pp. 110-21.

McLuhan, Marshall. 1964. *Understanding Media: The Extensions of Man*. New York: Signet.

Miki, Roy (ed.), 1989. "Syntax Equals the Body Structure: bp nichol in Conversation with Daphne Marlatt and George Bowering" *Line* 6, (Fall), pp. 22-44.

Miller, Stephen E. 1994. "The Grid: Living in Hollywood North" in Paul Delany (ed.) *Vancouver: Representing The Postmodern City*. Vancouver: Arsenal Pulp Press, pp. 282-94.

Minghella, Antony (dir.), 1996. *The English Patient*. Walter Murch (ed.). Saul Zaentz/Miramax, TigerMoth/Miramax, USA.

Mozley, Anita Ventura. 1979. "Introduction to the Dover Edition" in Eadweard Muybridge, *Muybridge's Complete Human and Animal Locomotion. All 781 Plates from the 1887 Animal Locomotion*. 3 vols. New York: Dover.Vol. 1, pp. vii-xxxviii.

Mukherjee, Arun. 1994. *Oppositional Aesthetics: Readings from a Hyphenated Space*. Toronto & Cardiff: Tsar.

Mundwiler, Leslie. 1984. *Michael Ondaatje: Word, Image, Imagination*. Vancouver: Talon Books.

Muybridge, Eadweard. 1979. *Muybridge's Complete Human and Animal Locomotion. All 781 Plates from the 1887 Animal Locomotion*. 3 vols. New York: Dover.

Nadel, Ira B. 1997. *Various Positions: A Life of Leonard Cohen*. Toronto: Vintage Canada.

Nichols, Allan (dir.), 1983. *I Am A Hotel*. Canada.

Nichols, Bill. 2001. *Introduction to Documentary*. Bloomington: Indiana University Press.

Nodelman, Perry M. 1980. "The Collected Photographs of Billy the Kid" *Canadian Literature*, pp. 68-79.

Novak, Amy. 2004. "Textual Hauntings: Narrating History, Memory, and Silence in *The English Patient*" *Studies in the Novel* 36.2, (Summer), pp. 206-28.

Novas, Himilce. 1996. *Mangoes, Bananas and Coconuts*. New York: Berkley Publishing.

Oleksijczuk, Denise Blake. 2002. "Haunted Spaces" in Stan Douglas (ed.) *Every Building On 100 West Hastings*. Vancouver: Contemporary Art Gallery/Arsenal Pulp Press, pp. 96-116.

Ondaatje, Michael. 2007a. *Divisadero*. Toronto: McClelland & Stewart.

Ondaatje, Michael. 2007b. "The fine line between memory and story" *The Irish Times Weekend Review*, (Sept. 29), p. 7.

Ondaatje, Michael. 2002. *The Conversations. Walter Murch and the art of editing film*. Toronto: Vintage Canada.

Ondaatje, Michael. 2000. *Anil's Ghost*. London: Bloomsbury.

Ondaatje, Michael. 1999. *Handwriting*. New York: Alfred A. Knopf.

Ondaatje, Michael. 1998. *Coming Through Slaughter*. Toronto: Vintage Books.

Ondaatje, Michael. 1996. *The English Patient*. Toronto: Vintage Books.

Ondaatje, Michael. 1992. *The English Patient*. London: Bloomsbury.

Ondaatje, Michael. 1988. *In the Skin of a Lion*. London: Picador.

Ondaatje, Michael. 1983. *Running in the Family*. London: Picador.

Ondaatje, Michael. 1982. *Running in the Family*. London: Picador.

Ondaatje, Michael (ed.), 1979. *The Long Poem Anthology*. Toronto: The Coach House Press.

Ondaatje, Michael. 1976. *Coming Through Slaughter*. Toronto: Anansi.

Ondaatje, Michael. 1970a. *The Collected Works of Billy The Kid*. New York: W. W. Norton & Company.

Ondaatje, Michael. 1970b. *The Collected Works of Billy the Kid*. Toronto: House of Anansi.

Ortega Y Gasset, Jose. 1956. *The Dehumanization of Art: And Other Writings on Art Culture*. Garden City, New York: Doubleday & Company, Inc.

Pabst, G. W. (dir.), 1929. *Diary of a Lost Girl*. Perf. Louise Brooks. VHS. Kino Video, USA, 1990.

Pabst, G. W. (dir.), 1928. *Pandora's Box*. Perf. Louise Brooks. DVD. Golden Hollywood Video, USA, 2006.

Perloff, Marjorie. 1998. "*After Free Verse*: The New Nonlinear Poetics" in Charles Bernstein (ed.) *Close Listening: Poetry and the Performed Word*. Oxford: Oxford University Press, pp. 86-110.

Rentschler, Eric (ed.), 1990. *The Films of G. W. Pabst: An Extraterritorial Cinema*. New Brunswick: Rutgers University Press.

Rifkind, Candida. 2002. "Screening Modernity: Cinema and Sexuality in Ann-Marie MacDonald's *Fall on Your Knees*" *Studies in Canadian Literature/Etudes en Litterature Canadienne* 27(2), pp. 29-50.

Roberts, Gillian. 2002. "'Signs of Omission': *The English Patient*, THE ENGLISH PATIENT, and the Critics" *Essays on Canadian Writing* 76, (Spring), pp. 195-215.

Rosenblum, Naomi. 1984. *A World History of Photography*. New York, London & Paris: Abbeville Press.

Rothgerber, Miriam A. "'Speaking One's Soul's Truth': Reading Michael Ondaatje's *Running in the Family* and Harold Brodkey's *This Wild Darkness: The Story of My Death* as Fictionalized Memoirs" Proceedings of the 2003 Hawaii International Conference on Arts and Humanities. 12 July 2005, http://www.hichumanities.org/AHproceedings/Miriam%20Rothgerber.pdf.

Rothman, William. 1998. "The Filmmaker as Hunter: Robert Flaherty's *Nanook of the North*" in Barry Keith Grant and Jeannette Sloniowski (eds.) *Documenting the Documentary: Close Readings of Documentary Film and Video*. Detroit: Wayne State University Press, pp. 23-39.

Rushdie, Salman. 1999. *The Ground Beneath Her Feet*. London: Jonathan Cape.

Schlüpmann, Heide. 1990. "The Brothel as Arcadian Space? *Diary of a Lost Girl* (1929)" in Eric Rentschler (ed.) *The Films of G. W. Pabst: An Extraterritorial Cinema*. New Brunswick: Rutgers University Press, pp. 80-90.

Scobie, Stephen. 1994. "The Reading Lesson: Michael Ondaatje and the Patients of Desire" *Essays on Canadian Writing* 53, (Summer), pp. 92-106.

Sobieszek, Robert A. 1999. "Abstract Machines of Faciality: The Dramaturgical Identities of Cindy Sherman" *The Ghost in the Shell: Photography and the Human Soul 1850-2000: Essays on Camera Portraiture*. London: MIT Press, pp. 170-283.

Solnit, Rebecca. 2003. *Motion Studies: Time, Space and Eadweard Muybridge*. London: Bloomsbury.

Somacarrera, Pilar. 2004. "*A Madwoman in a Cape Breton Attic*: Jane Eyre in Ann-Marie MacDonald's *Fall on Your Knees*" *Journal of Commonwealth Literature* 39.1, pp. 55-75.

Sontag, Susan. 1979. *On Photography*. London: Penguin.

Sontag, Susan. 1978. *On Photography*. New York, NY: Dell Publishing, Inc.

Sontag, Susan. 1977. *On Photography*. Harmondsworth: Penguin.

Sontag, Susan. 1977. "In Plato's Cave" *On Photography*. London: Penguin, pp. 3-24.

Talbot, William Henry Fox. 1969. (rpt. 1844-46 ed.) *The Pencil of Nature*. New York: Da Capo.

Tatum, Stephen. 1982. *Inventing Billy the Kid: Visions of the Outlaw in America*, 1881-1981. Albuquerque: University of New Mexico Press.

Testa, Bart. 1994. "He Did Not Work Here For Long: Michael Ondaatje in the Cinema" *Essays on Canadian Writing* 53, (Summer), pp. 154-67.

Thomas, Peter. 1980. *Robert Kroetsch and His Works*. Toronto: ECW Press.

Thorne, Matt. 2002. "*Journey into Fear* and Melville's *The Confidence-Man*" in Stan Douglas, *Journey into Fear*. London: Serpentine Gallery & Köln: Verlag der Buchhandlung Walther König, pp. 19-23.

Turci, Monica. 2001. *Approaching that Perfect Edge: A Reading of the Metafictional Writings of Michael Ondaatje* (1967-1982). Bologna: Pàtron.

Turner, Peter. 1987. *History of Photography*. Twickenham: Hamlyn.

Virilio, Paul. 1998. "A Topographical Amnesia" in Nicholas Mirzoeff (ed.) *The Visual Culture Reader*. London & New York: Routledge, pp. 108-24.

Watson, Sheila. 1959. *The Double Hook*. Toronto: McClelland & Stewart.

Weaver, Mike. 1998. "Artistic Aspirations and the Lure of Fine Art" in Michel Frizot (ed.) *A New History of Photography*. Bonn: Könemann, pp. 185-95.

Witte, Karsten. 1990. "China and Yet Not China: *Shanghai Drama* (1938)" in Eric Rentschler (ed.) *The Films of G. W. Pabst: An Extraterritorial Cinema*. New Brunswick: Rutgers University Press, pp. 167-74.

York, Lorraine. 1988. *"The Other Side of Dailiness": Photography in the Works of Alice Munro, Timothy Findley, Michael Ondaatje, and Margaret Laurence*. Toronto: ECW Press.

"Canadian Studies" Series titles

No.18 – André MAGORD, *The Quest for Autonomy in Acadia*, 2009, ISBN 978-90-5201-476-0

No.17 – Carmen CONCILIO & Richard J. LANE (eds.), *Image Technologies in Canadian Literature. Narrative, Film, and Photography*, 2009, ISBN 978-90-5201-474-6

No.16 – John-Erik FOSSUM, Paul MAGNETTE & Johanne POIRIER (eds.), *The Ties that Bind. Accommodating Complex Diversity in Canada and the European Union / Ces liens qui unissent. Gérer la diversité au Canada et dans l'Union européenne*, 2009, ISBN 978-90-5201-475-3

N° 15 – Pascale VISART DE BOCARMÉ et Pierre PETIT (dir./eds.), *Le « Canada inuit ». Pour une approche réflexive de la recherche anthropologique autochtone / "Inuit Canada". Reflexive Approaches to Native Anthropological Research*, 2008, 195 p., ISBN 978-90-5201-427-2

N° 14 – Serge JAUMAIN et Nathalie LEMARCHAND (dir.), *Vivre en banlieue. Une comparaison France/Canada*, 2008, 189 p., ISBN 978-90-5201-415-9

N° 13 – Nick NOVAKOWSKI & Rémy TREMBLAY (eds.), *Perspectives on Ottowa's High-tech Sector*, 2007, 270 p., ISBN 978-90-5201-370-1

N° 12 – Jean-François DE RAYMOND, *Diplomates écrivains du Canada. Des voix nouvelles*, 2007, 164 p., ISBN 978-90-5201-346-6

N° 11 – Claire OMHOVÈRE, *Sensing Space. The Poetics of Geography in Contemporary English-Canadian Writing*, à paraître, ISBN 978-90-5201-053-3

N° 10 – Caroline ZÉAU, *L'Office national du film et le cinéma canadien*, 2006, 463 p., ISBN 978-90-5201-338-1

N° 9 – Serge JAUMAIN et Paul-André LINTEAU (dir.), *Vivre en ville. Bruxelles et Montréal aux XIXe et XXe siècles*, 2006, 375 p., ISBN 978-90-5201-334-3

N° 8 – Madeleine FRÉDÉRIC et Serge JAUMAIN (dir.), *Regards croisés sur l'histoire et la littérature acadiennes*, 2006, 195 p., ISBN 978-90-5201-333-6

N° 7 – Zilá Pierre ANCTIL & Zilá BERND (eds./dir.), *Canada from the Outside In / Le Canada vu d'ailleurs*, 2006, 294 p., ISBN 978-90-5201-041-0

N° 6 – José GOTOVITCH et Anne MORELLI (dir.), *Contester dans un pays prospère. L'extrême gauche en Belgique et au Canada* (titre provisoire), à paraître, ISBN 978-90-5201-309-1

N° 5 – Britta OLINDER (ed.), *Literary Environments. Canada and the Old World*, 2006, 246 p., ISBN 978-90-5201-296-4

N° 4 – Madeleine FRÉDÉRIC, *Polyptyque québécois. Découvrir le roman contemporain (1945-2001)*, 2005, 176 p., ISBN 978-90-5201-096-0

N° 3 – André MAGORD (dir.), *Adaptation et innovation. Expériences acadiennes contemporaines*, 2006, 274 p., ISBN 978-90-5201-072-4

N° 2 – Robert C. THOMSEN and Nanette L. HALE (eds.), *Canadian Environments. Essays in Culture, Politics and History*, 2005, 316 p., ISBN 978-90-5201-295-7

N° 1 – Serge JAUMAIN & Éric REMACLE (dir.), *Mémoire de guerre et construction de la paix. Mentalités et choix politiques. Belgique – Europe – Canada*, 2006, 316 p., ISBN 978-90-5201-266-7